Cambridge Elements ☰

Elements in Contemporary Performance Texts
edited by
Senior Editor
Fintan Walsh
Birkbeck, University of London
Associate Editors
Duška Radosavljević
Royal Central School of Speech and Drama, University of London
Caridad Svich
Rutgers University

THE POETICS OF PERFORMANCE DIAGRAMS

Andrej Mirčev
Berlin University of the Arts

CAMBRIDGE
UNIVERSITY PRESS

Shaftesbury Road, Cambridge CB2 8EA, United Kingdom

One Liberty Plaza, 20th Floor, New York, NY 10006, USA

477 Williamstown Road, Port Melbourne, VIC 3207, Australia

314–321, 3rd Floor, Plot 3, Splendor Forum, Jasola District Centre,
New Delhi – 110025, India

103 Penang Road, #05–06/07, Visioncrest Commercial, Singapore 238467

Cambridge University Press is part of Cambridge University Press & Assessment,
a department of the University of Cambridge.

We share the University's mission to contribute to society through the pursuit of
education, learning and research at the highest international levels of excellence.

www.cambridge.org
Information on this title: www.cambridge.org/9781009517461

DOI: 10.1017/9781009446235

First published 2024

A catalogue record for this publication is available from the British Library.

ISBN 978-1-009-51746-1 Hardback
ISBN 978-1-009-44622-8 Paperback
ISSN 2753-2798 (online)
ISSN 2753-278X (print)

Cambridge University Press & Assessment has no responsibility for the persistence
or accuracy of URLs for external or third-party internet websites referred to in this
publication and does not guarantee that any content on such websites is, or will
remain, accurate or appropriate.

The Poetics of Performance Diagrams

Elements in Contemporary Performance Texts

DOI: 10.1017/9781009446235
First published online: May 2024

Andrej Mirčev
Berlin University of the Arts
Author for correspondence: Andrej Mirčev, a.mircev@udk-berlin.de

Abstract: This Element considers the concept of performance diagrams and shows their historical, epistemic and aesthetic functions in theatre and dance. In three sections, this Element surveys the architectural model by Vitruvius, the woodcut of Marlowe's *Doctor Faustus*, Aby Warburg's *Mnemosyne-Atlas*, the spells and drawings of Antonin Artaud, the performance *Paradise Now* (the Living Theatre) and the choreography *I Am 1984* (Barbara Matijević). Demonstrating that diagrams can be applied to multiply dramaturgical and performative trajectories, the Element reviews their relevance for performance-making, analysis and documentation. This Element argues that diagrams provide new methodological and analytical tools for theory, practice-based research and archiving, while at the same time enabling reflection on the intersections between poetics and politics. Focusing on the potentiality of diagrams to cut through representation and dichotomies, this Element affirms the visual, corporeal and spatial dimensions of performance-making. In doing so, it elucidates the significance of diagrammatic thinking for performance and theatre studies.

Keywords: diagrams, spatiality, memory, politics, cosmology

ISBNs: 9781009517461 (HB), 9781009446228 (PB), 9781009446235 (OC)
ISSNs: 2753-2798 (online), 2753-278X (print)

Contents

Introduction

Examining the histories, epistemic functions and the shifting aesthetic paradigms of diagrams in their relationship to text and performance, this Element illuminates how diagrammatic practices have been pivotal to theatre- and performance-making in different cultural and sociopolitical contexts. Their ability to act as graphic and schematic tools for creating spatial and visual constellations turns diagrams into distinctive instruments for mediating transformations of ideas into real-world situations. Due to their potentiality to serve both as dramaturgical models for performance-making and as archives/scores, diagrams multiply epistemic and aesthetic perspectives on theatrical and choreographic creation.[1]

Confronted with the reduction to the medium of speech, theatre has incessantly engaged in reinventing its theatricality and performativity. If performance-making is not only about the spoken word, representation and fiction, it could be asked: what is the role of materiality, visuality and spatiality? Is it possible to formulate a non-hierarchical model of performance departing not from the primacy of the speaking subject but from multisensorial scripturality[2] of graphic traces and affective embodiment? One of the Element's aims is to shift the focus from the fictional worlds of textual representation to the materiality, visuality and spatiality of performance. However, this does not imply that I consider fiction and materiality as opposite sides of performance-making. Instead, I would like to demonstrate their blending which, as I will argue, can be comprehended diagrammatically.

Overshadowing other means of expression, spoken and recited texts have dominated classical forms of Western dramatic performance, particularly genres like tragedy. With the dramatic text serving as the primary impulse for the play of theatrical signs, the materiality of stage and performance were most of the time suppressed. In other words, spatiality, visuality and corporeality were subordinated to the primacy of speech and text. Published in 1498 (the Latin translation by Giorgio Valla), Aristotle's *Poetics* became a seminal text influencing the theories, dramaturgies and performance practices over the last 500 years. For the Greek

---

[1] Elsewhere, I have written extensively on *diagrammatic dramaturgy* organized around generating 'the move/translation of concepts to concrete and lived/danced experiences' (2021: 56).

[2] Taking up and deconstructing the notion of the *pharmakon* as it appears throughout Plato's dialogues, Jacques Derrida identifies 'the exclusion and devaluation of writing', which is a direct consequence of the opposition of diction to scription as well as Plato's denigration and refusal to attribute written text with the ability to convey the truth (1981: 158). This ontological degradation of writing, Derrida shows, is foundational to a set of dualisms such as soul/body, good/evil and light/darkness that underpin the metaphysical, theological, poetic and political structures of the Western world. In the case of theatre and performance, the dualistic and logocentric ontology results in the opposition stage/audience, presence/absence, voice/body, text/performance and performance/documents.

philosopher, every tragedy has six parts: 'story, stats of character, wording, thinking, *spectacle,* and song-making' (2005: 27, my emphasis).

According to this typology, opsis (ὄψις Gr. Orig.) – the optical and visual element of performance or spectacle – is insignificant and subdued to the 'agency of speech' (Aristoteles, 2006: 49) Such a logocentric organization of (dramatic) theatre with the speaking subject at the centre resulted in the substitution of the actor's body with a sign. The emphasis on speech generated a condition in which the viscerality of performance is subsumed to the semiotic function, resulting in the priority of acting styles that aim to create an illusionary double of the world. In other words, the actor's task in the naturalistic and realist theatre was to generate a fictional situation on stage. Drawing on Hans Thies-Lehmann, it could be argued that by downgrading opsis, Aristoteles created the condition in which 'the staged event is basically superfluous' (2016: 1).

Asserting that diagrams complicate any system of knowledge revolving around dichotomies such as space/time, text/image, stage/spectator and body/ mind, the ensuing sections discuss the potentiality of diagrammatic models to foster discursive operations that surpass clear-cut definitions and institutional, disciplinary or cultural hierarchies. At the same time, their capacity to expose what a performance can be and become makes the diagram an effective dramaturgical tool for connecting texts, scripts and other means with their potential scenic embodiments in the future.

Starting with the architectural diagram in the *Ten Books on Architecture* by Vitruvius, Section 1 examines the relation between theatre and astrology that is further reconstructed in Marlowe's *Doctor Faustus*. In Section 2, the focus shifts to the cartographic and diagrammatic methodology underpinning the *Mnemosyne-Atlas* as it was developed by the art historian Aby Warburg in the late 1920s. In this section, I will also survey the affective aspect of performance diagrams by analysing the spells and drawings of Antonin Artaud. Section 3 assesses the performance *Paradise Now* (the Living Theatre) and the lecture performance *I Am 1984* (Barbara Matijević), asking if it is possible to converge poetics with the politics of performance diagrams.

Drawing on Thea Brezjek's and Laurence Wallen's argument from their book on the model as performance, I will demonstrate that diagrams in theatre and dance display the poetic process of performance-making.[3] For Brezjek and Wallen, the concept and practice of the model, as it appears in scenography and architecture, plays a major role in the design and, thus, is an essential tool

---

[3] The notion of poetics, which I will use throughout this Element, refers primarily to the material and conceptual process of artistic creation in literature, visual arts, music and theatre. As such, the theoretical and analytical concept of poetics can be utilized to comprehend how a specific work of art or (in our case) performance comes into being.

for creation. Arguing that model-making and modelling processes (to this, I add diagramming) are vital to research and explore the formal elements of performance, Brezjek and Wallen highlight the immanent poetic aspect. Linked, as they write, 'to invention and imagination more than the pragmatic need of the scenographer and the architect (. . .) models are physical and conceptual instruments of the cosmopoetic (world-making) act – they are able to comprise entire worlds' (2018: 11).

Accordingly, *The Poetics of Performance Diagrams* is an attempt to interrogate how diagrammatic practices can shed new light on performance-making. As it will be examined, one conceptual feature of diagrams is the capacity to unfold reflection that moves away from regimes of representation and dualistic paradigms. For John Mullarkey, the diagram is an 'indefinite relation of subject-world intertwining' and, therefore, has the power to manifest 'as an indefinite set of materialised 'betweens': between symbolic representation and iconic presentation, discourse and inscription, matheme and patheme, digital and analogue, geometry and art, internal representation and external picture, audience and artwork' (2006: 159–180). Understood as moving form endowed with the potentiality to unsettle dominant systems of representation, diagrams in this Element are envisioned as expressive instruments of *poetics without hierarchies*.

A significant quality of (performance) diagrams is their proximity to topological and cartographic modalities. Both maps and diagrams make visible graphic constellations between images and text. At the same time, neither maps nor diagrams function merely as representations but rather establish a dynamic, relational spatiality that accentuates processuality. Reflecting on the diagrammatic impulse and its relation with the concept of *poetic cartography*, the visual artist Simonetta Moro demonstrates the *carto-aesthetic* qualities of diagrams.[4] The diagrammatic and the cartographic impulse intersect in the possibilities of performing the line, 'which include the geometric line, the written line, the graphic line' (Moro, 2021: 115).

Analysing the handwritten notations of Walter Benjamin – many of which are diagrammatic – Moro shows how these graphic constellations of words and symbols challenge hierarchies and linearity, exposing a free-floating series of connections. The nonlinear way of organizing ideas and concepts in many ways resembles drawing and mapping. The shift to diagrammatic and cartographic practices of writing (instead of the more traditional, linear mode), I argue, sets in motion a *graphic force* which, at the same time, reads as a rehabilitation of the

---

[4] The concept of *poetic cartography* results from Moro's refusal to separate the political from the poetic. She writes: 'Ultimately, it will be demonstrated that a new, radical poetic cartography is necessary to illuminate issues at the forefront of current world crises and events, from mass migration to ecological collapse, from new nationalisms to a postborder world' (2021: 139).

'graphic signifier' and enables the rediscovery of the materiality and viscerality of writing (Derrida, 1981: 110).

Drawing a parallel with the postdramatic poetics of theatre and performance, such a (diagrammatic) move signifies the liberation of affectivity and sensuality from the closures of representation and the dictatorship of phonocentric theatre. In other words, the *re-turn* to diagrams will enable me to revisit the performance's spatial, corporeal and visual elements (the *opsis*.) As Thies-Lehmann shows, for Plato *opsis* 'is fundamentally subject to error', and hence must be distinguished from the 'inner logicticity' of the intellect being the only instance at which truth can be thought (2016: 27).

The hostility towards visuality – and here we could add not just for visuality but also towards the visceral and the materiality of performance – is the consequence of Plato's dualism that had created an epistemic and ontological schism between the physical world and the realm of ideas. The effect of this *double split* between mind and matter is the denigration of senses and sensuality. Due to their explicit relationality, diagrams show the potential to act as poetic devices of entanglement, visualizing knowledge, moving bodies across binary divisions and generating new social realities through aesthetic events.

With this in mind, I propose to define the concept of performance diagrams invoking the *relational poetics* theorized by the French writer, poet and philosopher Édouard Glissant. Analysing the poetics that were held responsible for the entrance of French literature into modernity, he identifies the *poetics of depth*, the *poetics of language-in-itself* and the *poetics of structure*. Yet, there is, Glissant writes: 'another unnoticed, or rather evaded (poetics) that we shall call a poetics of relation' (1997: 26). As a form of geographical writing that aims to untangle the colonial matrix, Glissant grounds his concept of relationality in the graphic and spatial elements of writing. Retracing the dangerous journey of slaves from the African continent to the Americas, he revisits the confrontation between the powers of the written word and the impulses of orality.

In an argument against the notion of roots, Glissant returns to the *rhizomatic thought* charted by Gilles Deleuze and Félix Guattari. His concept of the 'Poetics of Relation' thus challenges any fixed concept of identity and contrasts it with nomadic thinking. The poetics of performance diagrams is premised on a similar model of thought organized around errant[5] movements. In other words, the poetics I would like to formulate in the following sections traverses the dualities built around representation, identification and territoriality.

---

[5] As Glissant shows, the great founding books of communities such as the *Old Testament*, *Odyssey*, *Aeneid* or the African epics 'were all books about exile and often about errantry.' A passionate desire to rebel against roots acknowledging 'the rhizome of a multiple relationship with the Other' that becomes manifest in the poetry of Arthur Rimbaud. See Glissant (1997: 15–16).

Another theoretical impulse to articulate a poetic model of performance creation based on the diagrammatic is the work of the German philosopher Sybille Krämer. Intending to deconstruct the binary opposition between text and image, she conceived the concept of 'operational imagery' (*Operative Bildlichkeit*, Ger. Orig.). Interpreting the diagram as a cultural technique and mode of thinking, she radicalizes Derrida's project on grammatology by substituting it with *diagrammatology*.[6] According to Krämer, the diagrammatic comes from the interaction between imagination (*Einbildungskraft* Ger. Orig.), the eye and the hand. It is a spatial relation that 'mediates between the sensual and the sense' (2009: 105).

Closely related to the concept of operational imagery is Krämer's notion of *text-visuality* (*Schriftbildlichkeit*, Ger. Orig.). It implies a synthesis of visibility, manageability and flatness, all of which are attributes of the diagrammatic. This, we could say, enables us to comprehend the spatiality and visuality of writing and thinking. Demonstrating that diagrams are not only elements of visualization but instruments of experimentation, Krämer argues that they convey new epistemic constellations between concepts and senses. In the closing paragraphs, she writes that the diagram becomes a *stage* on which we can locate the 'liaisons between seeing and thinking' (2009: 117). By identifying the theatre stage as such a locus where the act of seeing becomes intertwined with thought, this Element asserts poetic and conceptual proximities between performance and the diagrammatic.

At this point, the reader might wonder how diagrams can *actually* be related to theatre, dance and performance. What are the possible conceptual and theoretical intersections between diagrams and performance practices? Can we deploy them to examine the redistribution of sociopolitical forces within a performance? Furthermore, can diagrams unfold knowledge about interdisciplinary and transcultural performance moving across medial, geographical and cultural borders? What can they disclose about the archiving strategies within performance and theatre studies?

In diverse disciplines such as mathematics, psychoanalysis, art history and information sciences, diagrams play a decisive role in argumentation by visualizing epistemic constellations between speculative and empirical data. While they are theorized in philosophy and in semiotics by authors such as Charles S. Pierce and Fredrik Stjernfelt, diagrams have been almost entirely absent from theatre and performance studies. One notable exception is the research by the

---

[6] Although Krämer evokes a 'linguistically oriented turn to visuality' in philosophy that can be attributed to Derrida, she argues that because of a certain 'iconophobia', the pictorial dimension of writing has been obscured (2009: 97).

theatre scholar Irit Degani-Raz who published two articles focusing on the reconstruction of performance diagrams in the work of Samuel Beckett.

With the intention of expanding the semiotics of theatre, Degani-Raz argues 'to include diagrams within the scope of application of the icon to this art' (2008: 133). Doing so enables her to interpret Beckett's short play *Come and Go* as a spatial manifestation of a mathematic-like diagram, according to which the three female figures with the distinctive colour of their costumes (violet, red, yellow) have the function of indexical signs. More precisely, 'the three actresses on stage are *icons* of three women in the fictional world', which implies that the diagram epitomized in the theatrical text reads as an axiom of the geometry of human existence (2008: 142). Degani-Raz emphasizes the epistemological mechanism underpinning diagrammatic iconicity and suggests a structural homology between the fictional world and reality. Furthermore, Beckett's theatrical diagram indicates a system of permutations grounded in a speculative logic of possible worlds.

In her second article from 2021, she moves the focus to diagrammatic reasoning within theatre. Herewith, she 'exposes previously unrecognized logical procedures that are activated during the process of deciphering a theatrical work' (2021: 2). Such an undertaking sheds light on new formal ways of understanding the spatial aspects of dramatic texts. Examining the central role of iconicity allows her also to explore the creative ways by which playwrights and directors have incorporated diagrams into their plays and performances. When considering diagrams from a semiotic standpoint, as suggested by Degani-Raz, we must reflect on their double aesthetic and epistemic functions.

Surveying diagrams within a threefold discursive and conceptual framework – historical, epistemic and aesthetic – *The Poetics of Performance Diagrams* illuminates how theatre and dance emerge from the intersections of knowledge, culture and imagination. With an emphasis on the different forms within theatre and performance, diagrams in the following sections are examined as architectural schemata, a book illustration, drawings on paper, a booklet/poster and choreographed traces written on a paper/blackboard. Hence, they are reflected in their capacity to serve as poetic displays relating acts of diagramming to performance-making.

This Element is structured around three sections with two central case studies diffracted through a multifocal theoretical and interpretative apparatus. Methodologically, it connects close reading with iconographical analysis (Sections 1 and 2) and performance analysis (Section 3). Accordingly, the themes are arranged chronologically, displaying historical examples and comparing them with case studies from the twentieth and twenty-first centuries.

The specific selection of the analysed diagrams is motivated by the intention to illuminate their heterogeneity and hybridity while showing different manifestations across different historical and cultural contexts. Following a diachronic trajectory, I am focusing on case studies in which the diagram is the central and prominent element of the performance. Except for the last example, which concerns a dance performance, the other five elucidate the epistemic and aesthetic relationship between theatre and ritual. What conceptually connects them is the manifestation and survival of hermetic and cosmological symbolism expressed, documented and disseminated through diagrams.

Since this is not a comprehensive and exhaustive study but rather a preliminary attempt to initiate a transdisciplinary discussion about the graphic and diagrammatic performance dimensions, numerous diagrams are not considered. For instance, what is left out[7] is the diagram of Stanislavski's system from 1935 and Richard Schechner's graphical configuration of performance from 1977. Performance diagrams are especially widely present in various choreographic practices, such as the works of Trisha Brown, Rudolf Laban[8] and William Forsythe. Without the objective of providing a definite classification and analysis of diagrams in dance, I am reflecting on their possibility to articulate a different, non-dualistic approach to the entanglements of dance, writing and image.

Section 1, *Performance Diagrams and the Poetics of Cosmological Space*, discusses the Roman theatre plan formulated by the Roman architect Marcus Vitruvius. In a close reading of his book *Ten Books on Architecture*, I will show how Vitruvius invokes a diagrammatic scene outlining the geometrical plan of the theatre. As the only book on architectural theory to have survived from Antiquity, it influenced cultural imagination and performance space design during the Renaissance. Since Vitruvius' diagram echoes the Platonic concept of the microcosm outlined in the dialogue *Timaeus*, the analysis reconstructs the cosmological diagram embedded in the architectural and spatial model. I argue that this model plays a pivotal role in comprehending performance space's history, architecture and *cosmopoetics*. At the same time, it potentially sheds new light on the relationship between ritual and performance.

In the second part of the section, the focal point shifts to the iconographical analysis of the woodcut given on the title page of the 1620 edition of Marlowe's *Doctor Faustus*. It depicts the magus standing within a circular structure embellished with symbols of the Zodiac and the seven planets. He holds

---

[7] Both Stanislavski's and Schechner's diagrams are presented in a visual essay by Richard Gough in the volume *On Diagrams & the Diagrammatic*. See Gough (2022).

[8] As Paola Crespi shows, in Laban's case the productive tension between movement and writing gives birth to a diagrammatic rethinking of the 'vexed relationship between writing, movement and corporeality' (2022: 108).

a magician's rod in his right hand and, in his left, an open book. Interpreting the image as *diagrammatic scene* aims to examine its relation to the cosmological model of theatre as described by Vitruvius. The comparison of the two diagrams (Vitruvius and Marlowe) will show overlapping points and it will elucidate the shift to early modernity. Analytically, the section cross-connects spatial theory (architecture) and cultural history with theatre studies, iconography and philosophy.

Section 2, *Transmission of Affects between Bodies and Images*, looks at the unfinished *Mnemosyne-Atlas* created by the art historian Aby Warburg in the 1920s. He made it intending to map image movements from Antiquity to the Middle Ages and their afterlives in the Renaissance. Centred around the notion of the 'Pathos Formula', designating the ability of images to capture and express extreme affective states, Warburg's *Atlas* is both a map and a diagrammatic device. As such, it navigates and retraces movements of images in and across bodies. Since Warburg focuses on the transhistorical motion of pictorial themes, the *Atlas* disrupts any fixed geographical and temporal division between the 'East' and the 'West'. Moreover, it brings to attention an interwoven and dynamic art and theatre history. In this section, I will argue that such a diagrammatic structure can be applied to performance and dance studies. Especially, if the aim is to rethink the dualism between performance/memory and shifts the research focus to translocal connections between different performance cultures.

Analysing the series of drawings that Antonin Artaud had devised from 1937 to his death in 1948, the second example in the section reveals the affective dimension of performance diagrams. Revaluating the mythological and ritual-istic aspect of Greek theatre and referring to the secret teachings of the Kabbalah and alchemy, Artaud performs his drawings believing they have the power of magic spells. I interpret these diagrams as an affective expression of embodied forces moving beyond the closures of representation. What is foregrounded is the capacity of diagrammatic poetics to unfold new corporeal scenarios and enable a different approach to text and performance-making. Together, the two case studies make visible the potentiality of diagrams to entangle performance cultures and thereby trespass the dividing lines between the East and the West.

Section 3, *Towards Sociopolitical Diagrams*, formulates a detailed analysis of the diagram circulated as a booklet and poster for the 1968 performance *Paradise Now* by the Living Theatre. It displays the figure of a man and of a woman. Their bodies are traversed with sentences and diagrammatic schemes written in Hebrew letters, Tantric symbols and hexagrams taken from the book *Ji-Ching*, an ancient Chinese divination text. Activating the diagram, the per-formers on stage engage in a corporeal action of forming letters with their bodies. Interpreting this theatrical situation as a diagrammatic act visualizing and embodying the script, I will demonstrate the intermedial transfer between the stage, the bodies and the text. Moreover, I will argue that the *Paradise Now* performance sets in motion a *revolutionary diagram*. It aims to traverse the distinction between the stage and the audience and blur the dividing line between art, activism and politics.

The second example in this section is the project *I Am 1984* from 2008 by the Croatian artist Barbara Matijević. It is a pseudo-scientific journey into the historical and cultural facts of 1984. As a performative multiplication of different narrative layers ranging from her autobiographical memories, the national history of socialist Yugoslavia (where she was born) and world history, the piece is choreographed as a lecture performance. With the focus on performing a diagram on paper, the choreography poetically blends visual traces with writing, speaking and movement. Drawing connections between personal memory, fiction, actual events from sports to the entertainment industry, media culture and advertising, Matijević uses the diagram to explore the digital age of hypertextual networks. In doing so, she engages the audience in an intricate narrative that reads as a social critique of the machinic enslavement and the tyranny of semiotic operations.

By analysing multiple manifestations of diagrams, this Element inaugurates a heterogeneous discursive trajectory that blends historical and cosmological aspects of performance-making with contemporary reflections about the politics of performance in the context of an accelerating algorithmic data flow. Traversing the boundaries between image, text and corporeality, the concept of the performance diagram proposes a non-hierarchical and nomadic poetics. Lastly, arguing against dualism, representation and the primacy of phonocentric fiction, the sections outline a performative territory haunted by affectivity and viscerality. In that way, this Element becomes a conceptual and speculative map to navigate the *chaosmosis* of performance creation.

1 Performance Diagrams and the Poetics of Cosmological Space

Written near the end of the first century BC, the book *De Architectura* by Marcus Pollius Vitruvius is one of the rare works on architecture to have survived from Antiquity. After the Italian scholar and Renaissance humanist Poggio Bracciolini discovered a copy of the manuscript from the ninth century at a monastery library in St. Gall (Switzerland), it became a vital source for artists, architects and writers, especially during the Renaissance. Dedicated to Caesar Augustus, *De Architectura* reads as a treatise on different elements of the theory and practice of architecture. For Vitruvius, architecture consists of three parts: the building, the construction of clocks and the mechanics. Prescribing that the architect must be educated in nine disciplines, he writes:

> To be educated, he (the architect) must be an experienced draftsman, well versed in geometry, familiar with history, a diligent student of philosophy, know music, have some acquaintance with medicine, understand the rulings of legal experts, and have a clear grasp of astronomy and the ways of Heaven. (2001: 22)

Before shifting the focus to the close reading of sections of the book 5 and 9 in which Vitruvius evokes one the first cosmopoetical diagrams of theatre, let us have a brief look at the second discipline which is necessary for the architect and that he lists after writing: drawing.

    While the architect and historian Indira Kagis McEwen writes that 'Vitruvius himself deliberately shunned drawing and resorted to graphic methods with much reluctance' I would dispute this statement, asserting that it sets the 'litteratus' (writing) and 'peritus graphidos' (drawing) in an opposition (2003: 32). Instead of reproducing such a binary reading, I would like to demonstrate that the practice of writing and drawing converge in the diagrammatic act as it puts the written sign and the visual trace into an interaction.

1.1 Staging the Zodiac

After he had analysed how the Greeks built their forums and basilicas, Chapters 3 to 7 are dedicated to the architectural construction of the theatre. Within the frame of our examination, let us first survey Chapter 6. Vitruvius writes:

> The plan of the theatre itself is to be constructed as follows. Having fixed upon the principal centre, draw a line of circumference equivalent to what is to be the perimeter at the bottom and in it inscribe four equilateral triangles, at equal distances apart and touching the boundary line of circle, *as the astrologers do* in a figure of the twelve signs of the zodiac, when they are making computations from the musical harmony of the stars. (1914: 146, added emphasis)

Invoking a geometric plan in which four equilateral triangles are inscribed in a circle, Vitruvius draws the analogy to astrologers who – interpreting the Zodiac – proceed just as Vitruvius describes (Figure 1). The splitting of the circle into twelve symmetrical parts serves them to map, calculate and constel-late the twelve celestial signs (Figure 2). At this point, we could become curious about the connection between astrology and the architectural plan of the theatre. Is it plausible to assert that cosmological concepts influenced the spatial poetics of performance? How are cosmology and astrology related to theatre?

    For Vitruvius, the knowledge of astrology is one of the nine disciplines. Drawing on the doctrines of Greek philosophers such as Pythagoras,

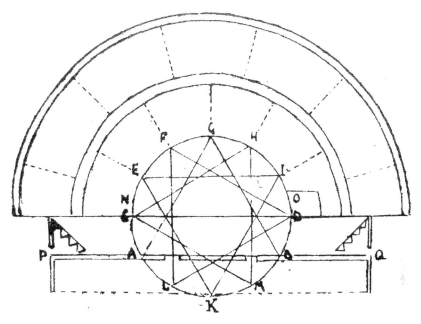

Figure 1 Vitruvius, model of the Greek theatre, design by Nikoleta Marković, courtesy of the artist

Democritus and Plato, Vitruvius sketches out his theory of the cosmos in book 9, which is dedicated to the construction of clocks. By the cosmos, he understands the general assemblage of all nature. It also implies the rhythmic movement of the stars organized into artificial constellations. In this part of the book, he gives an account of the significance of the number twelve, which corresponds to the twelve signs of the Zodiac.

While the knowledge of cosmological laws is the consequence of empirical observation and geometrical/mathematical calculation, the act of interpretation involves a work of poetic and pictorial imagination.[9] Regarding the specific shape of the Zodiac signs, Vitruvius makes it clear that each sign 'shows an image taken from nature, outlined in a pattern of stars among the twelve matched divisions of the belt' (2001: 109). As German literary scholar Sigrid Weigel contends, the Greek and Roman astrologers had turned the constellation of the fixed stars into a series of images connected to the figures of Greek

---

[9] In his analysis of patterns in Islamic architecture, Keith Critchlow asserts that the circle as a cosmological image with the twelve-fold division corresponds 'to zodiacal archetypes and, hence, to an annual cycle' (2011b: 61). As he shows, sacred rites and the architecture of temples are based on the knowledge of the anatomy of the cosmos. The primary number of the Zodiac (12) is a product of 4 and 3. Interpreted traditionally, 'these numbers symbolize the fourfold polarization of Universal Nature into the active qualities of heat and cold and the passive qualities of moistness and dryness' (2011: 58).

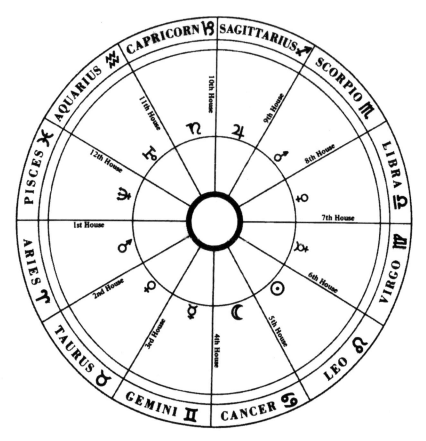

Figure 2 Twelve signs of the Zodiac, design by Nikoleta Marković, courtesy of
the artist

mythology (2015: 369). Thus, astrological patterns join empirical knowledge
with the poetic faculty and imagination.

One such poetic rendering of the Zodiac constellation can be found in
Chapter 5 (section 9), where we read:

> A Snake (Hydra), stretching along Virgo, Leo, and Cancer, twists back and
> binds together the line of stars, rearing its face up in the region of Cancer,
> holding up the Cup with the middle of its body hard by Leo, and setting down
> its tail, on which stands the Crow, at the hand of Virgo. The stars above its
> shoulders are of equal brightness. (Vitruvius, 2001: 114)

The act of turning groups of stars into animals (Leo, Cancer), human figures
(Virgo) or objects (the scales of Libra) shows that for the human being, this was
a way to make sense of the circular and repetitious movement of the planets and
the stars. Analysing the envisioning processes by which stellar constellations

were transformed into images – a process which is already evident in Vitruvius – Weigel shows how, with the triumph of Christianity since the sixth century, one can observe a 'tendency of de-imaging' (*Entblidlichung* Ger. Orig.), resulting in 'geometrical or diagrammatic figuration' (2015: 371–372).[10] I argue that the theatre plan that Vitruvius had laid out anticipates precisely such a diagrammatic configuration and ordering of performance space.

Asserting that 'a constellation is a graphical pattern which emerges from the interaction between points, lines and surface', Sybille Krämer and Christina Ljungberg explicitly refer to the structure of the Zodiac (2016: 3). This is the backdrop for their argument on the capacity of diagrams to unfold epistemic scenarios beyond the opposition of the iconic and the discursive, the figurative and the symbolic. In addition, they elaborate on the *diagrammatic scenario* according to which Zodiac constellations reveal characteristic features of diagrams. There are six such features: flatness, graphism, relationality, schematism, referentiality and usefulness. Cosmological diagrams displaying the Zodiac aim to order the celestial chaos, transforming it into a relational, graphic scheme.

With this in mind, I will now closer examine the plan of the theatre Vitruvius is presenting. Why is he modelling it as a cosmological/astrological diagram? By aligning the stage with the order of the heavens, Vitruvius highlights the necessity of the theatre space to be synchronized with the musical harmony of the stars. Thus, he not only postulates a connection between theatre architecture and nature/cosmos but suggests that the stage must be conceived as a ritualistic, sacred space mirroring the harmony of heavenly spheres.[11]

For McEwan, astrology and music overlap in the notion of the 'ratio' (or *logos* in Greek) signifying the harmonical structure of the heavenly and musical spheres. However, while McEwan contends that ratio – the divine measure of the cosmos – primarily involves language, I would challenge this assumption and assert that it results from a diagrammatic activity. One that joins the act of writing with that of drawing and connects the work of the architect to the practice of the astrologer and the musician. In other words, the cosmological scheme of the stage serves as a world-ordering tool with distinctive poetic qualities.

For further reflection on the significance of the cosmopoetic diagram in *De Architectura*, we have to consider the specific geometrical shape of the stage: the circle. As an expression and manifestation of the natural order, the round stage, which is divided into twelve parts, mirrors the spatiotemporal structure of

---

[10] Unless otherwise noted, all the translations from German are mine.

[11] We can be reminded that 'the Roman theatre was always a religious practice' (Wiles, 2003: 37).

the universe. Analysing how Vitruvius grounded his concept in the notion of astral religion, David Wiles writes:

> The Pythagorean principle that the ratios between musical notes correspond with ratios defined by the planets underpins his understanding of sound. Plato's assumption that the movement of the spheres creates a heavenly music too perfect for the human ear to apprehend, though rejected by Aristotle, was common currency in the Roman world. (2003: 183)

The scheme of the Zodiac thus becomes a backdrop against which he displays the organization of the theatrical microcosm. By urging the architect to work 'as the astrologers do', Vitruvius establishes what can be considered the first *diagrammatic scene* of theatre. Its proportions and ratio should reflect the geometrical laws and the mythological patterns governing and ordering the universe.

A concept that can further clarify why Vitruvius emphasizes the connection between the stage and the Zodiac is that of orientation. Art historian David Summers defines it as follows:

> The verb 'to orient' is from the Latin word for 'east' or 'dawn,' which in turn is from the meaning 'to rise,' closely related to 'origin.' The rising of the sun on the eastern horizon thus has the deepest associations with renewal and rebirth, still preserved, for example, in the name of Christian celebrations of Easter, which descends from similar roots. (2003: 180)

In addition to orientation, Summers discusses the idea of 'alignment' that – together with orientation – constitutes social space's elements. 'By means of a social space', so Summers: 'Our alignment is made part of a larger embracing order, part of a cosmos' (2003: 183). In other words, it is a fundamental means by which our physicality is set in relation to our world and culture. Although Summers does not explicitly refer to the passage in which Vitruvius lays out the astrological diagram of the theatre, he shows that the Roman architect gave clear instructions for the alignments of cities, temples and theatres.

'Once the forum has been laid out,' so Vitruvius, 'then a site should be selected for a theatre for watching the entertainments on the feast days of the immortal gods. This site should be as healthy as possible' (2001: 65). The architect must avoid a southern alignment because of the air and wind, which can burn up and dry up the spectator's body. As we can read from this passage, the concepts of alignment and orientation play a vital role in defining the topology of theatre. At the end of book 4, Vitruvius prescribes a similar alignment regarding the altar. It should face the east and always be placed on a lower level than the statues in the temple. In that way, Vitruvius prescribes an astral and solar orientation both for the temple and the stage.

In an attempt to show that Greek tragedy was a spatial construct structured around the binary of the east/west opposition David Willes demonstrates how the theatrical space was neither neutral nor empty, but that the dramatic text lent meaning to the space. The performances in Athens were created 'within and in response to a network of pre-existing spatial relationships' (1997: 4). Arguing that academic research on drama and tragedy has been preoccupied with time rather than space, he relates Greek drama to the visual arts. Consequently, such an epistemic perspective leads him to conclude that the performance space of Greek theatre follows the doctrines of cosmological orientation and alignment principles.

By reconstructing the visual and spatial axes of the theatre of Dionysus, Wiles points out the 'alignment of god, door and altar' and makes it clear that there is a symbolic relationship between 'the space of tragic performance and the space of sacrifice' (1997: 58). The spatial consequence of such a topographic *orientation towards the dawn* is that the visual focus in many Greek tragedies is the altar or the tomb. Grounding his argument on modern archaeological findings as well as in experiments in acoustics, he shows that the 'visual and the acoustical focus are intimately related' (1997: 70).

Drawing on Vitruvius, Wiles demonstrates that by laying out his plan of the theatre space, the Roman architect 'chose to give equal cultic significance to Apollo and Dionysus' (1997: 43). This we might read as an attempt to establish a twofold focus: the visual and the acoustic. Hence, when structuring the theatre diagram as a circular space divided into twelve parts, Vitruvius repeats the cosmological schemata inherited from the Greeks. It implies that the performance space is organized around the four cardinal points that highlight the rhythmical motion of the sun and the stars.

Yet, it would be a mistake to assume a continuity between the Greek and Roman theatres. While the difference must not be overlooked, a more comprehensive analysis is beyond the scope of this Element. The difference is the 'Greek sensitivity to landscape, versus a Roman determination to dominate nature' and

> The logic of astral thinking does much to explicate the semicircular Roman form. The powerful diameter line which divides actors from the audience is associated with the binary relationship of day and night, summer, and winter, waxing and waning moon; only half the zodiac, and half of each planetary sphere, can be in the visual field of human beings at any one time of year. (Wiles, 2003: 184)

Diagrams organize knowledge by relating words, concepts and images and can be seen as speculative and ordering devices. By interpreting the signs of the Zodiac as a diagrammatic and ordering scenario, Krämer and Ljungberg argue,

'The signs of the Zodiac have a purpose. By organizing the stellar chaos, they create possibilities for geographic orientation on earth' (2016: 5). Reproducing the scheme of the Zodiac, the architectural diagram thus serves both as an instrument of orientation/alignment and a poetic tool for establishing the *sacred topography of the stage.*[12]

Although we do not have an exact sketch by Vitruvius, the image of the male body enclosed in a circle and a square is one of those iconic representations that have fuelled the visual imagination over the last two millennia. In book 3 (Chapter I), he gives a precise account of the temple design and how it depends on the symmetrical relation between the different architectural parts. In that sense: 'without symmetry and proportion there can be no principles in the design of any temple' (2001: 72). Drawing an analogy with the proportions of, as he calls it, 'the well-shaped man', Vitruvius resorts to geometrical figures to conceive his argument. Here again, we encounter the shape of the circle and the square: 'And just as the human body yields a circular outline, so too a square figure may be found from it' (2001: 73).

Similar to the Zodiac diagram that helps us imagine the configuration of the stage, the emphasis on circularity in the well-shaped man's diagram aims to establish a relation between the body and the cosmos. It implies a connection between the microcosm and the macrocosm represented in the constellations of the Zodiac. Both the theatre diagram and the diagrammatic rendering of the Vitruvian man bring to the fore a poetics that revolves around the idea formulated in Plato's book *Timeaus*. For Plato, imitating the rounded shape of the universe 'the gods bound two divine circuits into a spherical body, which we now call the head' (2009: 35) What the Greek philosopher herewith establishes is an analogy between man-universe, which would become central for the occult and hermetic teachings from Antiquity to the present day.

In *Timaeus*, Plato presents a mathematical structure of cosmos that was foundational to scientific, literary and artistic imagination. Departing from a complicated system of correspondences that essentially was a mixture of empirical, astrological and mythological knowledge, books such as the *Corpus Hermeticum* and Plato's *Timaeus* insisted on the ontological parallels and similarities between the sublunar and the celestial world. In an attempt to

---

[12] Analysing the motif of the Zodiac circle that has been discovered in the mosaic floors of six ancient synagogues in Palestine, archaeologist Jodi Magness writes that scholars 'have suggested that this motif represents a kind of liturgical calendar, or that it had magical, cosmic, or astrological significance' (2005: 7). For Magness, the central placement of the Greco-Roman god in a central position in synagogues from the fourth and fifth centuries, testifies to the fact that 'Jews and Christians appropriated each other's visual language and symbols in their attempt to claim the temple' (2005: 14). In other words, the images of the Zodiac were intended to evoke the temple in Jerusalem.

decipher the precise meanings of Plato's intricate thoughts, Calcidius, a fourth-century philosopher who translated Timaeus from Greek into Latin, integrated twenty-five diagrams into the comments to the text.

Examining cosmological and astronomical diagrams from the Middle Ages (tenth to fourteenth centuries), art historian Kathrin Müller combines art historical analysis with the discourse of the history of science to show how the diagram functions as a 'visual figure of understanding' (2008: 34). As such, it is not only instrumental for the ordering of knowledge but it comes also with an aesthetic surplus, merging the mathematical and empirical worldview with theology, mythological imagination and the ritualistic practice.

The geometry of the circle and the square function to align the body with the four cardinal points that serve as an axis of orientation both concerning the four sides of the world and to the motion of the heavenly spheres. According to McEwan, the Vitruvian man can be seen as a metaphysical proposition as it 'is also a ritual formula' (2003: 162). The ritualistic value of the Vitruvian diagram signifies the idea according to which 'the body is always seen as engaged with its place and ultimately with the hierarchy of places (topology) within a unified cosmic framework' (Vesely, 2002: 31). The analogy of body and architecture, body and cosmos, establishes a precise relation between Zodiacal phenomena and zones of the human body. During the Middle Ages, this resulted in countless manuscripts on medicine and astrology, many of which contained diagrams revealing the correspondences between the parts of the body and the Zodiac. One such example is the diagram/image of the *Anatomical Man* in the manuscript entitled *Très Riches Heures du Duc de Berry* by the Limbourg Brothers (1412–1416).

Reflecting on the Vitruvian account of the origins of architecture, Karsten Harries underscores that there is a link between the upright gaze directed at the stars (which is a vertical orientation) and the act of building. This leads him to the conclusion about the verticality of humans manifesting in a 'transfigured spiritual architecture' that has a spherical shape and mirrors the macrocosm/microcosms analogy. (2002: 153) Neil Leach's article on *Vitruvius Crucifixus* follows a similar line of thought, linking the spiritual and sublime with the question of the body and architecture. Here, the focus is on discussing the connection between representations of the Vitruvian man and the crucified Christ. He illustrates his thesis with a diagram of the Vitruvian man that can be found in Cesare Cesariano's edition of Vitruvius' book and Brunelleschi's wooden crucifix in the church of Santa Maria Novella in Florence. In the conclusion, Leach argues: 'Yet the Renaissance was as much about the Christianization of a Vitruvian tradition as it was about the Vitruvianization of a Christian one' (2005: 213).

The architectural performance diagram and the image of the Vitruvian man disclose how both the space and the body relate to the cosmos and, thus, are metaphysically aligned with the heavenly spheres and the harmonical motion of the stars. Arguing that this cosmology had a significant influence on the visual and poetic imagination, it could be asked if there are other iterations of the diagram in different historical and cultural contexts. One such example indebted to the Vitruvian cosmological model can be identified in the frontispiece of Christopher Marlow's *Doctor Faustus*.

The stage on which we see the magus depicted in the woodcut is defined by a circle on the floor. Drawing a parallel with the architectural plan in Vitruvius' writings, *Doctor Faustus* might be envisaged as an example of another performance diagram. In both cases, the centrality of the circle yields an expanded reflection of its significance. Indebted to the astral religion of the Egyptians, the mystical mathematics of the Pythagoras and the astrology of Chaldeans, 'Plato's cosmic circle', as Wiles designates it, originates from the circular dance around the altar (2003: 168).

Although theatre and dance historians cannot precisely date the moment when Greeks began to perceive analogies between the circular dance of the chorus and the cosmic order, we can assume that images of dancing gods and dancing stars 'were born into the light of classical Athens on currents of mythopoetic thought' (Miller, 1986: 23). In a detailed examination and close reading of the surviving texts from Antiquity and medieval times that address the structure of the cosmos and relate it to the dance of the chorus, James Miller shows how such animistic skies (appearing, for instance, in Homer's *Iliad*) are essentially: 'Poetic skies'. On their backdrop, dance and performance 'would first make sense as an image of cosmic order' (1986: 24).

Applying these ideas to our examination, it seems credible to attribute an *immanent poetic power* to the Vitruvian and Faustian performance diagram. If the diagram we encountered in Vitruvius can be envisaged as the first example of its kind, then the scene with the magus depicted in the woodcut that we will analyse in the next section displays the afterlife of the cosmological circle. It repeats and reframes the analogy between the macrocosm and the microcosm expressed poignantly in the esoteric formula: 'As above, so below'. On the other hand, standing at the threshold of early modernity, Marlowe's diagram signifies the final days of Vitruvian cosmology. It prepares the stage for the heliocentric revolution and the rationalistic conception of spatiality and science, signalling the demise of magical thinking premised on analogy and similarity.

1.2 Diagramming Demons

The claim I would like to put forward in this section is that diagrammatic operations in Marlow's drama underpin the performance of magic rituals and are present in the text, not only in the woodcut. *Doctor Faustus* enables me to expand my reflection on the intersections between theatre, ritual and cosmology. First, I will show the *poetic afterlife* of the Vitruvian diagram and second, how the cosmological and astrological knowledge became somewhat of a *dramaturgical movens* in the dramatic literature of the Elizabethan period. Although various theatre, cultural and literature scholars have thoroughly analysed the play's historical and aesthetic facets, to the best of our knowledge, none has attempted to examine the concept of the diagram and its relation to astrology and the necromantic ritual. Before engaging on a close reading of the dramatic text, I will focus on the visual depiction of the famous frontispiece.

Holding an open book in his left hand, the damned theologian stands in a circle. The floor in the small room is shown as a geometric grid composed of rectangular forms. The circle in which the magus stands is decorated with signs of the Zodiac and the seven planets, sometimes wrongly interpreted as hieroglyphs.[13] In his right hand, the magician holds a stick pointing to one of the signs in the circle. His gaze is directed at a grotesque, black creature outside the circle. The demon is portrayed with a pair of wings and a tail in the form of a spiral (Figure 3). Other visible elements are a model of the globe hanging in the left corner and next to Faust's head, a shelf with a box and a circular form that can be identified as a compass. Another cross is positioned right above the demon. In the background, we see a window. Without too many visual details, the woodcut locates the conjuring scene of the play in Faust's study room. More precisely, the image captures the very moment when Mephistopheles appears to the magus in scene III.

From the play, we learn that Faust turned to occult and magical practices after he renounced theology. The astrological diagram depicted on the floor plays a vital role. It comes to the fore not only with regard to the circle but can also be reconstructed from the text. According to Tom Mcalindon, *Doctor Faustus* is grounded in two traditions related to astrology. The first one is linked with 'witchcraft, demonism, and idolatry', while the other is associated 'with the astronomer's entirely laudable attempt to comprehend the divine order of the universe' (1994: 384–385).

---

[13] In his essay on the performative elements in the drama, Andrew Sofer notes that 'Indeed, the title page of the 1616 edition of *Doctor Faustus* (reprinted thereafter) shows the magician standing in a circle marked by hieroglyphs' (2009: 4). Apart from the mistake he makes regarding the hieroglyphs, Sofer elaborates how the practice of conjuring operates within the register of citation. Accordingly, performativity is a kind of magical altering of reality through the power of the word, one that channels what might well be called an occult force.

The Tragicall Hiſtoy of the Life and Death

of Doctor Fauſtus.

With new Additions.

Written by *Ch. Mar.*

LONDON,
Printed for *Iohn Wright*, and are to be ſold at his ſhop without
Newgate, at the ſigne of the Bible. 1620.

Figure 3 Title page of a late edition of Christopher Marlowe's *Doctor Faustus*
(1620) with a woodcut illustration of a devil coming up through a trapdoor.
Wikimedia Commons

In scene VII, Faustus is curious to know:

> Come, Mephistopheles, let us dispute again and
> Argue again of divine astrology.
> Tell me, are there many heavens above the moon?

Are all celestial bodies but one globe,
As the substance of this centric earth?

(2003: 368)

The dialogue between the cursed magician and the demon unfolds as a lesson in cosmology/astronomy. It presents the reader with the Renaissance doctrine of 'the seven planets, the firmament, and the empyreal heaven' (Marlowe, 2003: 369). The magic circle decorated with symbols of the Zodiac and the seven planets, together with the model of the globe positioned next to Faustus' head, point to the centrality of the cosmological discourse. Displaying the knowledge of the heavens, the text establishes a diagrammatic scene, connecting theatre explicitly with cosmology and the ritual.

Having the role of a predecessor who will transmit not only the geometrical knowledge of Greek and Hellenistic antiquity (embodied in the symmetry and harmony of circles and squares) but also the astrological tradition of Chaldeans and Egyptians, the revival of Vitruvius during the Elizabethan Renaissance had tremendous consequences for the arts and culture in England. In her analysis of the reception of Vitruvius by John Dee and Robert Fludd, Frances Yates illuminates how the books on architecture had provided them with an episteme that was mystical and hermetic but, at the same time, scientific and technological. Referencing Vitruvius and Agrippa, Dee 'equated the Vitruvian man with the magical cosmological man' (Yates, 1969: 39). Hence, the circle of the Zodiac turned into a demonic square with the magus diagramming and conjuring *the regent of perpetual night*, who rules over morning light in the east and appears as Venus.

Written to investigate Renaissance astrological principles and apply them to significant cosmological allusions of the Elizabethan and Jacobean dramatists, Johnstone Paar shows to what extent and with what significance the playwrights drew upon the astrological doctrines of their time. As he argues, Marlowe found the astrological proclivities of Faustus stated in the English *Faustbook*, his primary literary source for the play. 'It will be noticed,' so Paar: 'That in the process of his conjuration Faustus has recourse not only to incantations, prayers, sacrifices, and theological names, but also to astrology. (. . .) Into his magic circle, therefore, through which he shall raise spirits, Faustus has cast certain characters of the signs and the planets' (1971: 34).

After rejecting philosophy, medicine, theology and the sciences, we encounter Faustus turning to the practice of magic with the ambition to make man live eternally. He wants to achieve this 'by picking up a book of magic':

These metaphysics of magicians
And necromantic books are heavenly,
Lines, circles, schemes, letters, and characters –
Ay, these are those that Faustus most desires.

(2003: 348, emphasis added)

The necromantic books the magician wishes for are known as grimoires, magic manuals containing ritualistic formulas, images and schemes to summon angelic and demonic forces.[14] Can this be the reason for Marlowe to use phrases like 'lines, circles, schemes', thereby implicitly highlighting the diagrammatic structure of such books? Is it plausible to assert that diagrams play a decisive role in the performance of conjuration? Can we think of them as ritualistic, dramaturgical and poetic tools?

The circle adorned with symbols of the Zodiac and signs of the seven planets, together with the grimoire on the left and the wand in Faustus' right hand, display primary magic instruments. As one of the simplest geometrical forms, the circle defines the area in which the performance of conjuration takes place. Therefore, it is not surprising that it is centrally displayed on the frontispiece. As Tom Mcalindon observes: 'in many productions of the play, Faustus' magic circle is boldly and centrally represented on the stage floor' (1994: 391).

In scene III, Faustus enters the circle to summon the demon. It is described as follows:

> Within this circle is Jehovah's name,
> Forward and backward anagrammatized,
> The abbreviated names of holy saints,
> Figures of every adjunct to the heavens,
> And characters of signs and erring stars,
> By which the spirits are enforced to rise.
> Then fear not, Faustus, but be resolute,
> and try the uttermost magic can perform.
>
> *(2003: 354)*

These cryptic statements allude to a specific ritualistic practice of ceremonial magic with which Marlowe was obviously familiar.[15] Already in scene I, he gives us a clue by referring to Heinrich Cornelius Agrippa, the sixteenth-century German Renaissance theologian and occultist who wrote an influential study on ceremonial magic (*Three Books of Occult Philosophy*), in which he presented a synthesis of astrology, numerology, alchemy and the medieval Kabbalah.[16]

While it is absent from the circle depicted on the woodcut, Jehovah's name is accentuated in the text. As such, it determines the magic ritual in which Marlowe had situated the play. According to Elizabeth Butler, 'a great and

---

[14] For detailed historical research on grimoires, see Davies (2009).

[15] As John Mebane argues, 'Marlowe utilizes material from the Renaissance occult tradition' (1992: 16).

[16] In the text, we read: 'On sweet Musaeus when he came to hell, Will be as cunning as Agrippa was, Whose shadows made all Europe honour him' (Marlowe, 2003: 350).

almost impenetrable mystery had indeed gradually grown up around the name which to us seems the most familiar of all, even though its pronunciation has shifted in our own day: Jehovah or Jahweh' (1949: 40). Represented by four letters of the Hebrew alphabet, JHWH (יהוה) – known as the tetragrammaton – it plays a fundamental role in kabbalistic rituals. As a powerful formula, it is used in ceremonial magic to perform the invocation of angels and demons.

In that way, 'Cabbalism has never ceased to exert an incalculable influence upon occultists of every description' (Butler, 1949: 42). In his analysis of Faustus as a Renaissance magician, William Blackbourn shows that he is practicing a type of magic that unites 'Hermetic magic with Cabbalist magic' (1978: 4). The tradition can be traced back to the writings of Giovanni Pico della Mirandola, who, together with Agrippa, is another central figure of Renaissance philosophy, magic and occultism. Hence, when Faustus invokes the formula of Jehovah, he turns to the Kabbalah as a source of spells and divination techniques for conjuration rituals.

By rejecting (Christian) theology and turning to magic and occult practices grounded in astrology and Kabbalah, Faustus discards the teachings of the Bible. Instead, in scene V, he receives several conjuring books that enable him to raise up spirits whenever he wants. Presenting him with such a book, Mephistopheles says:

> Hold, take this book. Peruse it thoroughly.
> The iterating of these lines bring gold;
> The framing of this circle on the ground
> Brings whirlwinds, tempests, thunder, and lightning.
> *(2003: 365)*

Among the books Faustus obtains from the demon, a book on astrology is singled out: 'Now I would like to have a book where I might see all characters and planets of the heavens, that I might know their motions and dispositions' (2003: 366). The dismissal of theology affirms a ritualistic practice grounded in astrological and kabbalistic diagrams composed of *lines, circles and schemes.*[17]

If the thesis regarding the role of diagrams is plausible, we could further examine the specific nature of writing departing from the books Faustus uses to perform his ritual. Drawing on the research by Owen Davies, it could be said that 'the very act of writing itself was imbued with occult or hidden power', and that writing was primarily 'a tool of magic' (2009: 2). At the same time, the

---

[17] Tom Mcalindon writes that 'Faustus's turning from divinity is similarly signaled by an emphasis on astrology' (1994: 386).

performance of writing plays a significant role in the text. One of the most theatrical moments in the play is the scene when Faustus is cutting his arm:

> Lo, Mephistopheles, for love of thee
> I cut mine arm, and with my proper blood
> Assure my soil to be great Lucifer's
> Chief lord and regent of perpetual night.
>
> *(2003: 362)*

Yet, as the blood congeals, Faustus cannot write anymore and must wait until Mephistopheles returns with the fire. Only then can he resume signing the contract and promising his body and soul to the *Prince of the East*. As readers, we are thus turned into witnesses of a performative and corporeal form of scripture. It affects the body, leaving it wounded and with scars.

The fact that the medium of writing can be considered vital for the magical ritual is indicated on the woodcut as well. While the magus is holding the open grimoire in his left hand, in his right hand, we see him operating with a stick (magic wand) directed at one of the symbols in the circle. As we may refer to it, the *deictic gesture* performed with the help of the wand recalls both writing and reading. The fact that it points to the symbol of the planet Mercury (☿) might seem incidental. Yet, having in mind the specific astrological and ritualistic context of the play, this requires a more precise explanation.

Associated with the fastest planet in our solar system (Mercury), the symbol to which Faustus directs the wand represents the god Hermes in Greek mythology and the Egyptian god Thoth. According to Davies, 'Thot was thought to be the inventor of writing and mathematics and therefore the patron god of scribes and administrators. As the founder of the written word, it stood to reason he was also a supreme master of magic' (2009: 11). Magical thoughts and practices are displayed here as closely connected to writing. In the case of the damned necromancer, the performance of magic comes into being as an imprint of bloody traces on a scroll.

The significance of Mercury, symbolizing the practice of magic, can be traced back to Agrippa's *Three Books on Occult Philosophy*, whose 'importance as a source for the Faust legend' must be considered (Lehrich, 2003: 1). In Chapter XXX, Agrippa observes that whatsoever is found on the world is made according to the rule of the planets and that the 'occult virtue' has its source in the influence of Mercury, the planet associated in traditional astrology with communication and travelling (Agrippa, 2021: 106). In light of these ideas, the gesture of Faustus pointing to the symbol of Mercury visually expresses the intertwinement of writing, performance and magic.

For Jacques Derrida, the mythological figure Hermes-Mercury-Thoth stands for the double and contradictory nature of writing, operating in the space of difference between mythology and scientific logos. With regard to its polysemantic constitution, this figure is the 'god of calculation, arithmetic, and rational sciences' and 'also presides over the occult sciences, astrology and alchemy. He is the god of magic formulas that calm the sea, of secret accounts, of hidden texts: an archetype of Hermes, god of cryptography no less than of every other -graphy' (1981: 93). If viewed through such interpretative optics, the scene with the magus in the circle holding a book and pointing to a sign representing the god of writing – being at the same time the god of science and of hermetic magic – supports reflection on the medial conditions of the ritualistic performance. It becomes visible both as a space *of* writing and space *as* writing.

The play's reference to lines, circles and schemes signals the shift to hermetic practices and magic based on astrological divination and kabbalistic invocation. The result is another type of writing; one in which the borders between text and image are blurred. Although the woodcut does not provide the viewer with more visual details about Faustus' grimoire, we could speculate that the pages contained images of astrological magic, secret formulas and obscure signs that only made sense to someone initiated into the system of occult codes and their intricate symbolism. As Frank Klassen observes, 'the texts might also employ a mathematical figure such as a magic square. The image one was to carve or draw might be strange or disturbing and have no apparent relation to the more familiar signs of the Zodiac or planets' (2013: 14).

Examining the astrological image magic in medieval and Renaissance manuscripts, Klassen shows that it played a decisive part in the rituals. The theories about the agency of such magical images were derived from Neoplatonic cosmology. In particular, from the writings of philosophers Iamblichus and Proclus, who had directly influenced Renaissance authors such as Marsilio Ficion, Pico de Mirandolla, Agrippa or John Dee, the court astrologer of Queen Elizabeth. Is it, after all, credible to assume that the scene displayed in the woodcut relates the performance of Faustus to the practice of astrological image magic, which, in the given constellation, acquires a diagrammatic form?

Returning our analytical gaze to the woodcut, I will briefly examine the three other visual elements: the orthogonal grid on the floor, the globus hanging on the wall behind Faustus and the compass above the cross. While it might be evident that the globe and the compass establish a clear reference to geography, practices of mapping and orientation, the grid might be more puzzling. However, if we consider that the grid, the globe and the compass gain their visibility due to the graphic fabric of lines, it could be argued that together they make visible a 'theatrical geography' (Derrida, 1981: 69). Thus, the geometric apparatus appearing as a structure of orthogonal and circular lines creates a visual order but, at the same time, can be seen as an attempt to locate both the magus and the devil on the map and in the world.

Asking how and where Renaissance specialists on witchcraft and demonism situate demons within geographical space, Thibaut Maus de Rolley examines conceptions of spatiality in early modernity, merging demonological and geographical texts. If, as he argues, 'the Renaissance was the Age of Discovery, it was also the Age of Demonology' (2016: 180). In other words, the expansion of geographical knowledge and navigation tools (such as the compass) had a revitalizing effect on demonological imagination. The result was the emergence of the 'cosmography of the devil' (2016: 181). Furthermore, de Rolley shows how, during the Renaissance, demons were not confined to the other world but became mobile and capable of moving between the worlds. That is best exemplified in Mephistopheles' presence in the study room.[18]

Both the cosmographer and the demon can move around the globe and quickly change their place (a poetic quality attributed to the planet Mercury). In conclusion, de Rolley asserts that the merging of geography and demonology in a spatial system established on rational visuality (which is one of the defining features of advances in early modern optics) unfolds the 'poetics of diabolical space' (2016: 188). Such a spatial concept materializes in *Doctor Faustus* as a diagrammatic space oscillating between *lines, circles, schemes, letters and characters*.

In her reflections on diagrammatology, Sybille Krämer elaborates on the concept of the 'cartographic impulse' that serves her as a theoretical underpinning for the examination of various phenomena associated with graphic arrangements that are at the core of diagrams (2016: 87). Joining geographical and epistemic orientation, the cartographic impulse sheds light on the proximity of diagrams and maps. More precisely, a feature of the diagram is its potentiality to generate 'novel geometrical knowledge' by establishing a phenomenological relation between the eye and the hand, between perception and the conceptual mind (Krämer, 2016: 92).

Revealing that the diagram is a central discursive and conceptual object in the works of post-continental philosophy and authors such as Gilles Deleuze, Félix Guattari, Alain Badiou, François Laruelle and Giorgio Agamben, John Mullarkey argues that it provides a 'hermeneutics that is not representational

---

[18] After signing the contract with his blood, Faustus is curious to know: 'Where is the place that men call hell?' To this Mephistopheles answers: 'Under the heavens. (. . .) Hell hath no limits, nor is circumscribed in oneself place, for where we are is hell, and where hell is must we ever be. (. . .) All places shall be hell that is not heaven' (2003: 364).

but physical, a material hermeneutics of diagrammatic lines, planes, circles, and triangles' (2006: 10). When Faustus expresses his desire for necromantic, heavenly books traversed with *lines, circles, schemes, letters and characters,* isn't Marlowe anticipating precisely such a material hermeneutics? Moreover, can we consider the magus to embody an ambiguous and liminal figure standing on the border between the Renaissance and early modernity?

Mapping the intersecting areas of theatre, magic and perennial philosophy, Dragnea Horvath cross-examines the interrelatedness of aesthetic and epistemic patterns that had shaped the distinct physiognomy of Elizabethan performance culture, whose stages were populated with theatrical apparitions in the form of spirits, demons and angels.[19] Her analysis revolves around Shakespeare's views on the relationship between theatre and magic, and she looks for reverberations of the Neoplatonic philosophy of Ficino and Mirandola in John Dee's work on angelic and demonic powers, best mirrored in plays such as *The Tempest* and *Doctor Faustus*.

The idea and practices of theatre in early modernity underwent a semantic extension by incorporating cognitive experiences and forms of organizing know-ledge. In that way, 'the metaphor of the *theatrum mundi* turned into an explana-tory model of human life and the energy exchanges in the universe' (Horvat, 2017: 210). In this process resulting in a decentralized, plurifocal and relational theatre paradigm, the poetic mind merges with discursive and logical reasoning. Lastly, as the woodcut of *Doctor Faustus* suggests, the magus appears on a diagrammatic stage materialized around a scientific, rational and geometrical structure, which, at the same time, is poetic, mythological and diabolical. As a result, we can locate the performance diagram in these intersecting vectors of geometrical rationality and cosmological-ritualistic symbolism.

The circle in Faustus' study room frames the ritualistic context in which we can perceive the text and the performance. Being both a tool for ordering the heavens and a medium for invocation, the circle renders visible the *sacred and theatrical geography* into which the magus will summon the demon.[20] On the

---

[19] Addressing the semantic reconceptualization of the term *theatre* which in early modernity signified not only the play, the stage and the activity of performance but began to be associated with scientific and magic practices of experimentation and discovery, Horvath concludes that this enhanced the 'epistemological dimension' and led to the 'presentation of knowledge as *theatrum*' (2017: 32).

[20] After being silenced by the rise of Christianity, theatre – together with magic, Neo-Platonic and occult philosophy – flourished again during the Italian Renaissance. Such a parallel revival of theatre and magic coincides with the formation of a new episteme resulting in theatre getting closer to rituals. Horvath writes: 'Religious ritual is related to the sacredness of its performing space. Theatre makers, magicians and philosophers treated space in a comparable manner: the stage, the magical circle, the cabinets of wonders (...) were the special, well-circumscribed locations of their epiphanies' (2017: 53–54).

other hand, the globe, the compass and the geometrical structure of the grid – interpreted as apparatuses of early modern science and rationality – situate the text of the tragedy in a space of epistemic tensions, mutations and natural experimentations. The discursive juxtaposition of these two, distinct, but inter-related, spatial and semiotic regimes is the birthplace of Marlow's performance diagram.

Conclusion

The figure of the cosmological circle displaying the Zodiac was the focal point of this section. By bringing to attention the sacred space-time of theatre, I wanted to demonstrate the role of the diagram in creating the point of contact between ritual and performance. Although the cultural and historical difference between first-century BC Rome and sixteenth-century England must not be overlooked, we could identify a continuity of the astrological discourse and its significance for the performance of conjuration. In other words, not only has it survived, but it became one of the central themes in philosophy, science, magic and artistic practices in the Renaissance.

'Astrology,' writes Nicholas Campion, 'is therefore both the study of the ways in which significance for life on earth is located in celestial objects and the resulting practices. It may be speculative, but it can also be operative; it involves not only myth and ritual, but also action. It depends on rationales as various as divine intervention, celestial influence, or the notion of the sky as a script to be read for signs' (2009: xi). While it is primarily an act of empirical observation and calculation of the motion and the rhythms of heavenly objects (astronomy), the curious look directed at distant constellations is also the genuine source of imagination and, probably, one of the first impulses of mythological thinking and practices of storytelling.

The cosmic circle embellished with signs of the Zodiac, powerful names, and other ritual formulas – and manifesting as a performance diagram – is of central significance for religious and magic rites and the dramatic text, performance and scientific experiments. Finally, 'the theatre architecture inspired by Vitruvius' enabled 'the spectator to feel part of the macrocosm-microcosm dynamics' (Horvath, 2017: 33). It extended performance space into an epistemic space of experimentation and scientific operations. Suppose we can contend that Vitruvius' diagram prefigures the merging of poetic with epistemic and the ritualistic functions of theatre. In that case, Marlowe's diagram signifies the culmination of this transformation of the cosmological stage and anticipates the arrival of rationalistic, scientific space haunted by ghosts and apparitions that are summoned into the circle.

2 Transmission of Affects between Bodies and Images

The historical trajectory from Vitruvius to Marlowe in Section 1 outlined the complex relationship between cosmopoetical space, ritual practices and geographical/cartographic knowledge. The outcome of this examination was the argument that the merging of theatre, magic and science, as it occurred in early modernity and during the English Renaissance, reveals itself in the two performance diagrams. While this discursive operation aimed at reconstructing the *Theatrum scientiarium* and the *Theatrum philosophicum* in their diagrammatic intertwinement, in the first part of this section I will shift the focus on something that, echoing Giulio Camillo, can be denoted the *Theatrum memoriae*: a fluid and performative archive of images and memory.

Haunting the discourse of theatre studies, the antinomy liveness/memory still poses a significant methodological and theoretical challenge for historiographic research. This primarily concerns scholars, curators and artists dealing with ephemeral spectres of live arts that resist representation and commodification. Examining the potentiality to propose alternative approaches to archiving practices and procedures of documenting performance, theatre and dance, I argue that there is an overlooked, still insufficiently explored mnemonic dimension of diagrams. Affirming affectivity and searching for non-dualist models of theatre and performance memory necessitates a different notion of embodiment and visceral experience. Perhaps one that is grounded in relationality and affectivity.[21]

In the first part of the section, I will argue that the *Mnemosyne-Atlas* by Aby Warburg is such a methodological tool. Organizing art historical material and visual themes in a cartographic arrangement, he invented a genuine cultural technique to trace the repetition and transformation of visual forms and corporeal gestures across time and space. In doing so, Warburg founded an interdisciplinary historiographic method designed to examine trajectories of cultural exchange. Per se, the *Atlas* creates a dynamic epistemic condition mapping the sociocultural networks in which images and other cultural artefacts appear not as isolated aesthetic phenomena but as intertwined.

Heralded as one of the founding figures of iconology, Warburg anticipated the *iconic turn* which, in the last decades, resulted in the proliferation of a new discipline: Visual Studies. If, as Mischa Twitchin observes, the association of theatre with iconology might at first glance seem unexpected, the *Mnemosyne-Atlas* provides a vibrant model of 'theatrical iconology' (2016: 2). Rather than

---

[21] As Melissa Gregg and Gregory J. Seigworth write in their book, affects designate the capacity to act and be acted upon. As forces of intensities, they are manifestations of *in-between-ness* and can be invested to comprehend the relationality between humans and between humans and their environment (Gregg and Seigworth, 2010).

a simple return *to* the past, theatre iconology directs the researcher's attention to the return *of* the past, with the performance operating and moving between multiple temporalities. As such, it becomes an indispensable instrument to examine the afterimage and afterlife of performance. Although Rebecca Schneider does not refer to Warburg in her book on theatrical reenactments, the idea that the 'book engages the tangled temporalities and crisscrossed geographies' echoes the logic and method of the *Atlas* (2011:3).

Taking up the concept of the 'cartographic impulse' (discussed by Krämer) and examining it in the context of mnemonic transmissions of images and gestures, I will propose a diagrammatic understanding of the *Atlas*. Consequently, such a discursive manoeuvre aims to expose new historiographic tools that enact other tactics and means of documenting the phantoms of performance. This implies sharpening the critical gaze for *affective corporealities* and their turbulent movement between image and text. Hence, the tension reverberating between the iconic, the visceral register and the text becomes the next discursive site to consider the poetics of performance diagrams.

2.1 Diagrams of Intervals and Polarities

Aby Warburg's *Mnemosyne-Atlas* (*Bilderatlas-Mnemosyne*, Ger. Orig.) is a collection of 971 images clustered and organized to disclose the stylistic connections and relations between visual themes and objects.[22] He started collecting and arranging them in the aftermath of the horrors of the First World War and after being treated at a psychiatric clinic in Switzerland due to a nervous breakdown in 1922. For him, the *Atlas* was a tool for generating knowledge on the cultural transformation and migration of images, figures and corporeal gestures.

Instead of turning it immediately into a book, Warburg first curated an exhibition with the aim to display the reproductions of historical artworks from Greek and Roman Antiquity, mythology, divination objects from Egypt/Babylon and paintings of Renaissance authors. Eventually, to this day the *Atlas* remains unfinished and it is only due to the photographic documentation preserved at the Warburg Institute in London that researchers can reconstruct its contents. With an interest in determining the reverberation of visual schemata, Warburg wanted show how art history comes into being as a succession, repetition and dynamic survival/afterlife of forms. This characteristic technique of organizing fragments of images into thematic groups resembles the technique

---

[22] The exhibition *Aby Warburg: Bilderatlas Mnemosyne – The Original*, was shown at the Haus der Kulturen der Welt (HKW) in Berlin during the spring of 2020. It aimed at reconstructing the original, last known version of the *Atlas* and, for the first time since 1929, presented 'Warburg's original materials with some one thousand images on more than sixty cloth-covered panels' (Sherman, 2020: 8).

of collage, citation and film montage as it was practiced in the 1920s and 1930s by avant-garde artists such as John Hearthfield, Kurt Schwitters, Hannah Höch and filmmakers Sergei Eisenstein and Dziga Vertov.

For Sigrid Weigel, the *Atlas* functioned as 'a projection of the knowledge of images into a spatial constellation' (2013: 4). With it, Warburg created something he designates an 'iconology of interspace' (*Ikonologie des Zwischenraums*, Ger. Orig.), a discursive and heuristic instrument to bring images of different cultural origins into an epistemic constellation (Weigel, 2013: 5). It entails situating visual data into a network of historical and iconological connections. From an intermedial perspective, what is at stake is a diagrammatic configuration that merges pictures with texts, schemes and models.

For his 1905 lecture on Albrecht Dürer and the Italian Antiquity, Warburg prepared the first, miniature version of the *Atlas*. It had the form of a folder containing two reproductions of the images *Death of Orpheus* (one by Dürer and the other by an unknown Renaissance artist from Italy). In addition, it featured a third plate with three Greek vase paintings illustrating the same visual theme from the fifth-century BS and the reproduction of Jacopo Sellaio's painting *Orpheus and Euridice*. In 1909, Warburg delivered a series of seven lectures on the afterlife of Antiquity in the fifteenth-century Italian Renaissance. As Claudia Wedepohl observes, 'he tried a new form of 'genealogical' diagram to highlight both the migration and the interdependence of ideas, forming a complex network rather than a linear narrative' (2020: 15).

Although the chaotic events of the First World War and his mental health condition prevented him from developing the *Atlas* earlier, Warburg never abandoned it. Eventually, he returned to its creation in 1924, as soon as he was released from the clinic. The lectures series on the Renaissance in Florence, which he taught at the University of Hamburg, made him review his collection of visual material, manuscripts and books. Another impulse leading to the creation of the *Atlas* was the research and curatorial work on the history of astronomy and astrology that he was preparing for an exhibition at the planetarium in Hamburg in 1927.[23] As one of the first art historians to understand 'the significance of astrological-cosmological representations for the image-world of the Renaissance', Warburg expanded the traditional boundaries of art history and connected it to anthropology, psychology and religious sciences

---

[23] About the polarities between the rational and the mythological, Warburg wrote: 'Starting from the anterior Asiatic-Babylonian and Egyptian cosmology, followed by the Greek cosmology which in Alexandria becomes entangled in a twofold mythical-mathematical net, in the mirror of the simultaneous world of images it will be reflected how the ideas of order in the so-called Middle Ages and until Kepler were caught up in the struggle between the demon-fearing fortune-telling and exact celestial science' (Warburg in Naber, 1993: 11).

(Naber, 1993: 10). The migration and transformation of astrological and cosmological symbols are one of the central motifs the *Atlas* depicts.

The figuration of stellar and planetary constellations becomes the medium
through which it is possible to retrace the polarity between 'the religious and the
mathematical worldview (*Weltanschauung*, Ger. Org.)' (Warburg, 2012: 3).
According to Warburg, it is in this *space of polarity* where artistic creation takes
place. On the other hand, 'the surviving monstrous symbols of Hellenistic astrology' served as a cultural archive of corporeal images that bring to the fore
'representation of life in motion in the period of the Renaissance' (Warburg,
2012: 5–3). In short, as an inventory of energetic and affective gestures, the
Mnemosyne-Atlas proliferates a heuristic and diagrammatic convergence between
bodies, images and memory. Moreover, it enables the researcher to critically assess
and examine the *palimpsests of history*.

Following Gertrud Bing, a close collaborator and assistant of Warburg, it can
be asserted that astrological figures play a vital role in the concept of the 'Pathos
formula', one of the central concepts of his theory. As an expression of affectively
charged bodies, it marks the gestural and poetic repertoire of Antique shapes,
defining the visual patterns and narratives of art in the Renaissance and beyond.
Just like the pathos formula, 'astrology is a piece of pictorial knowledge that can
be traced from Antiquity to the Renaissance' (Bing, 1993: 21). Mapping the
afterlife of visual forms, Warburg argues that the 'unleashing corporeal expression' is kinetic, mnemonic and pictorial (2012: 4).

The diachronic migration of visual forms from one cultural and geographic
context to another is determined by the survival and reproduction of the affective
content inscribed into their materiality. This means that the pathos formula mediates, expresses and stores affective material. As the mnemonic repetition of images,
it is charged with intensive emotions and traumatic experiences (death, madness and
rape). With regard to temporality, it could be contended that 'Warburg's
Pathosformeln helps to see backward and forward in time' (Johnson, 2012: 18).

After this brief historical and epistemological survey, I will now examine some
of the contents of the *Atlas*. Panel A opens with two maps and one genealogical
tree of the Medici/Tornabuoni family. The first map depicts the sky with constellations of the Zodiac. It is a reproduction of the coloured etching on copperplate
from a Dutch book on celestial charts (seventeenth century). The second map,
placed below the first, displays the *Road of Cultural Exchange Routes Between
North. South and East*. Warburg devised this map to depict the historical transfer
of images in a motion from the south-east to the north-west[24] (Figure 4).

---

[24] In the preface to the collected manuscripts Warburg wrote on the *Mnemosyne-Atlas,* the editors
of the volume (Weigel and Treml) explain that his concept of the roads of cultural exchange

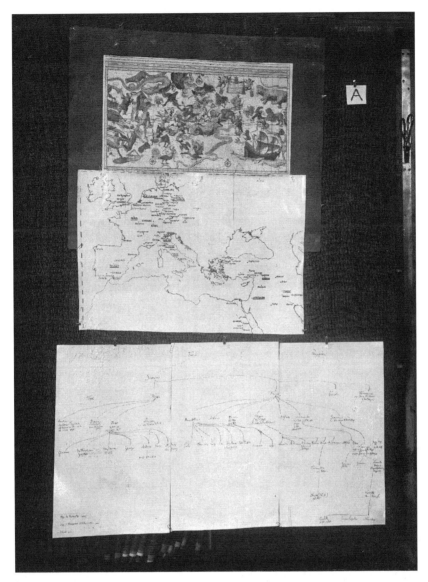

Figure 4 Aby Warburg, *Bilderatlas Mnemosyne*, 1927–1929, Panel A. London, Warburg Institute Archive

As one can read in the explanation, the panels envisage different systems of relationships in which humans are entangled: cosmic, earthly and genealogical. Here, we see one of the main features of Warburg's undertaking. The *Atlas* offers a 'visual-poetic form of knowledge' methodologically

---

(*Wanderstraße*n, Ger. Orig.) explore 'psychohistoric oscillations in the topography of the orient and the occident' (2010: 608).

situated in the interval between artistic imagination and rational/scientific calculation (Weigel, 2013: 9). As such, it mobilizes a space for thought connecting mathematical with magic thinking, unsettling 'the distinction between word and image', and thus radically blurring the borders between disciplines (Johnson, 2012: 20).

In the context of our inquiry, we could ask what status and function did theatre and the performing arts have for Warburg? Can its structure, contents and methodology be utilized for theatre, dance and performance studies? More precisely, what and how could the *Atlas* contribute to theatre and dance historiography? Reflecting on its methodology, theatre scholars Jan Lazardzig, Viktoria Tkaczyk and Matthias Warstat observe that theatre historians share with Warburg a similar longing to reconstruct the past not only from well-known sources such as institutional archives, museum collections or audiovisual documentation but also from 'seemingly marginal traces' (Lazardzig, Tkaczyk and Warstat, 2012: 1). Identifying lacunas in historiographic research, Warburg examined what moved human bodies in the past and how these movement patterns can be retraced and reactivated in the present. The marginal and ephemeral thus became the focal point.

Writing about theatre in the preface to the *Atlas*, Warburg makes a somewhat marginal claim about its mnemonic function, which – when enhanced through spoken words, images and architecture – can become an impulse to 're-experience human emotion' (2012: 5). Yet, as many of the plates illustrate, the corporeal, choreographic and performative elements are not peripheral but rather constitutive for the knowledge conveyed. For instance, scenes portraying the 'engrams of passionate experience' appear on plate 6 (Warburg, 2012: 3). Here, Warburg constellates the ritual dance in honour of the goddess Isis (Roman fresco, AD 50-75), the ritual funerary dance (Apulian mural painting, fifth century BC) with the dancing Maenads (Roman marble relief, AD 80–100) (Figure 5). What connect these images of dance are bodies displayed in the moment of intensive affects, the result of which are movements of disfiguration and intoxication. Hence, the gestural pathos formulas being 'intrinsically connected to the expression and arousal of extreme emotion' (Ruprecht, 2019: 128) expose the *iconological interval*. The image appears intertwined with the body in affect.

An example of how Warburg's concepts might apply to the study of dance and theatre history is the book *Poetics of Dance* by Gabriele Brandstetter, one of the first dance scholars to consider the pathos formula in performance and dance studies. In her words, 'pathos formulas are visual inscriptions of collective cultural memory – dynamograms – that still retain the imprint of cult ritual – at the origin of symbolic representation – and are constantly transformed anew in the receptive traditions of art' (2015: 26). Interpreted as a dynamic archive of

Figure 5 Aby Warburg, *Bilderatlas Mnemosyne*, 1927–1929, Panel 6. London, Warburg Institute Archive

cultural and corporeal memory, the pathos formulas shed new light on the formation and transformation of corporeal images and expressive gestures. Not only with regard to iconology and visual studies, but also concerning the analysis of movement patterns in dance and performance. Focusing on such representations of pathos formula in *fin de siècle* dance and the transformation of paradigmatic patterns of culture, Brandstter differentiates between two models of body imagery.

On the one hand, there is the 'Greek model', wherein the pathos formulas reactivate and reinterpret the patterns of nature that are modelled after the images of Antiquity. On the other, she identifies the 'exotic model': 'images of the body that evolved out of various encounters with foreign cultures, as well as with the Other in one's own culture' (2015: 28). These two models give way to poetics of free and expressionist dance embodied in the movements of Isadora Duncan, Loie Fuller, Rudolf von Laban and Gert Valeska. In short, Brandstetter's research poignantly shows how reading and seeing dance unfolds as a process of remembering. It is an art form that draws its mnemonic and iconic energies from the repertoire of cultural archives.

Created almost 400 years before the *Atlas*, Giulio Camilo's theatre of memory consists of images. With the *Atlas*, it shares a similar diagrammatic structure. For Camillo and Warburg, images carry an *affective agency* according to which they can animate bodies and souls. In Camilo's case, what determines their symbolism and meaning is the Neoplatonic notion of astral and solar magic combined with the teachings of the medieval Kabbalah.[25] According to Frances Yates, the memory images in his theatre have talismanic power, 'power to draw down the celestial influences and spiritus within the memory, such a memory would become that of the 'divine' man in intimate associations with the divine power of the cosmos' (1999: 155).

Camillo's outline of his *memory theatre*, which, unfortunately, survived only in the form of a diagram (reconstructed by Frances Yates in her book *The Art of Memory*), was propelled by the utopian ambition to represent and display all knowledge that could have been retrieved through existing texts and images. As Brezjak and Wallen observe, it was based on Vitruvius' theatre model, and it mirrored the Kabbalist *Tree of Life* with the ten divine emanations (sephiroth). Its function was to activate mnemotechnical operations 'based on linking images and words in specific locations within an overall physical environment' (2018: 52).

Apart from the fact that it exists *only* as a reconstructed diagram, Camillo's theatre model shows a diagrammatic structure comparable to Vitruvius and Marlowe. Operating more like an exhibition than a classical theatre setting with a fixed audience and a separate stage, the *Theatre of Memory* implies a peripatetic viewer. Spatially, it was designed as a circular structure divided by seven passageways representing the seven planets. As Yates writes, 'the solitary 'spectator' of the Theatre stands where the stage would be and looks

---

[25] Yates writes: 'Camillo brings the art of memory into line with the new currents now running through the Renaissance. His Memory Theatre houses Ficino and Pico, Magia and Cabala, the Hermetism and Cabalism implicit in Renaissance so-called Neoplatonism. He turns the classical art of memory into an occult art' (1999: 151).

towards the auditorium, gazing at the images on the seven time seven gate on the seven rising gates' (1999: 137).

The number seven connects the architectural structure of the theatre to the seven pillars of Solomon's House of Wisdom, which is an indication that Camillo had modelled his theatre mirroring the topology of the seven lower Sephiroth.[26] In this view, the mnemonic theatre replicates the order of the cosmos and turns the visitor into an active witness and participant of a performative cosmogony. In turn, he/she takes part in the visual mystery of creation and, by reactivating memory, can ascend back to the *limitless* Ain Soph (סוֹף אֵין, Hebr. Orig.), denoting the primal space 'in which all the worlds take birth' (Scholem, 1954: 297).

Comparing Camillo's *Theatrum memoria* to the *Mnemosyne-Atlas,* we can see that they intersect in a 'spatialized and theatricalized relationship between memory and recall' (Wallen and Brejzek, 2018: 55). More precisely, the production of mnemonic knowledge in both cases is performative and pictorial. In Warburg's *Atlas*, this is evident because the order of the panels is not fixed in a final constellation but can permanently be re-arranged and re-edited. Such a fluid structure resembles the poetics and dialectics of montage that is characteristic for the cinematic procedure of Sergei Eisenstein or the project on Parisian Arcades (*Das Passgenwerk*) by Walter Benjamin.[27] The conclusion to which George Didi-Huberman arrives is that the images in the *Atlas* are 'essentially montages of heterogeneous meanings and temporalities' (2017: 318). The same could be said for Camillo's memory theatre.

What can we then conclude about the diagrammatic agency of the *Mnemosyne-Atlas*? How can it be adapted for theatre, dance and performance historiography? It seems worth starting from 'the cartographic impulse' intrinsic to Warburg's project. Interpreted as a map that enables the user to achieve *orientation* and perform knowledge on the cultural history of migration of iconological patterns and images, the *Atlas* inaugurates a 'combinatory displacement of the images' (Didi-Huberman, 2017: 301). Thereby, it makes visible the interval of historical time as expressed in the iconology of interspace.

'This kind of diagrammatology', writes Mullarkey, 'follows the lead of Aby Warburg's anarchistic iconology or montage-collision. As a method of decontextualisation, it marginalises historical provenance and cultural context in favour of sheer appearance, uncovering kinships between images based on

---

[26] We shall return to the concept of the Sephirot examining it in more detail in the next section about the diagram for the *Paradise Now* performance.

[27] In her study on the parallels between Warburg's *Atlas* and Benjamin's *Arcades,* Cornelia Zumbusch observes that they share a similar idea regarding the connection between memory and images. In Warburg's case, the result is the 'opening of the space of thought' (*Eröffnung des Denkraums,* Ger. Orig.) and in Benjamin's, the notion of the 'dialectics at the standstill' (Zumbusch, 2004: 7).

their elements, their relative motions, and their juxtapositions in an almost cinematic manner' (2006: 181).

In her essay on the (meanwhile lost) map displaying the routes of the cultural transfer between the East and the West, and transition of images from Antiquity to the Middle Ages and the Renaissance, Claudia Wedepohl demonstrates its importance for the *Mnemosyne* project as such.[28] She argues that Warburg's 'historical model of the cultural transfer' implies a spatial and pictorial intertwining resulting in a *topographical representation* of images in motion (2005: 229).

Anticipating discursive practices such as the concept of 'crossmappings' (Elisabeth Bronfen), Warburg's *Atlas* provides the historian of theatre, dance and performance with a valuable heuristic instrument. Asking, 'why a given image formula bas been confiscated and re-interpreted in a particular way', Brofen argues that her method of crossmapping aims at 'uncovering developmental trajectories on the afterlife of cultural image formulas, which have often remained unnoticed' (2018: 5). Drawing attention to the fact that images haunt us from the past, Brofen revisits Warburg's cartography of the pathos formulas and, in doing so, exposes the affective experience of aesthetic transformation.

Such a discursive practice coinciding with the idea of 'spatializing the historical' serves the purpose of revealing conceptual and stylistic relations between artists and cultural events moving and transforming across time (Schmidt-Burkhard, 2012: 81). Or, put differently, the cartographic impulse immanent to the *Atlas* coincides with its diagrammatic trajectory. By focusing on the entangled, transcultural and transgenerational circulation of memory, a methodology inspired by the *Atlas* can be invested to look for parallel developments and histories of performance art and theatre.[29] What herewith comes to the fore is the potentiality of diagrams to unfold new epistemic configurations between the performing bodies, images and their archives.

Another diagrammatic constellation we can invoke to consider performance from the perspective of the affectivity and the circulation of images is the work of Antonin Artaud. What I specifically have in mind are Artaud's drawings, paintings and letters executed between 1937 and 1948. In these works, he develops hybrid text-image scenarios, rendering visible a disfigured corporeality traversed with affects and graphic traces of intense psycho-somatic suffering

---

[28] With regard to the diagram, her argument can be expanded to express epistemic and poetic formations performed by graphic traces in space. Furthermore, Wedepohl shows that the black plates with assembled images function as projections of complex historical developments 'on a flat surface' (2005: 229). Precisely, graphism, spatiality and flatness, as Krämer and Ljungberg remind us, 'are the resources for drawing, diagramming and writing' (2016: 4).

[29] One such project using a diagrammatic/cartographic method to examine local networks and historic connections of Swiss performance is the project 'Revolving Histories or Performance Art in Switzerland'. See Gebhardt Fink and Rust (2022).

and torture through drugs and electroshock treatments. Drawing a parallel with Warburg, who was also suffering from mental disorders and for whom the *Atlas* was a cure, Artaud's drawings and the spells were a medium of exorcism, as he believed that they protected him from the evil influences of demons.

As a visceral expression of social and psychic tensions, the pathos formula might be well attached to Artaud's intention to revive the cruelty, energetic intensity and pictorial memory of ancient and non-western rituals. Struggling with a deteriorating mental health in the times of historical crises such as the First and Second World War, Warburg's and Artaud's diagrams are symptoms of a battle to achieve orientation in an accelerating, transforming and collapsing world. For Didi-Huberman, the concept of the symptom he reconstructs in the work of Warburg designates the 'tension-laden process within images' (2017: 175). While this seems to be obvious in Warburg's case, it also applies to Artaud, especially when taking into account the circulation of affects in his writings, drawings and the spells.

2.2 The Spectacle of Tormented Flesh

Considered to be one of the most radical innovators of the twentieth century, Antonin Artaud has exerted a tremendous influence on contemporary theatre. Apart from directors such as Roger Blin, Jerzy Grotowski, Robert Wilson, Peter Brook, Richard Schechner or Judith Malina and Julian Beck, Artaud influenced the proliferation of new genres of the performing arts such as happening, performance and body art. Foremost, because he sought visceral means to counter the logocentric stage and the primacy of speech and language. Such a shift from a text-based model of performance entailed exploring and high-lighting other elements of theatre-making: body, image, space, light and sound. Also, it implies rehabilitating precisely the element Aristoteles deemed unworthy and irrelevant: the spectacle (opsis).

While Artaud is primarily known for his essays on theatre, short poems, letters and film scripts, he devised an opus of paintings and drawings. Analysing the spells he made from 1937 to 1939 and one drawing from the last years of his life (1948), I will show that they figure as performance diagrams. The spells and the drawing illuminate the intersections between theatre and ritual. They can also be considered as an expression of his critique of Eurocentric rationality grounded in the dualism between culture, nature and metaphysics.

Artaud's endeavour to reach beyond the limits of European culture parallels Warburg's anthropological interest for the indigenous cultures of the Pueblo tribe in New Mexico and the Hopi tribe in Arizona. This search for points of cultural exchange leads Warburg to the United States. In 1895/1896, he visited and photographically documented the two tribes. Later in 1923, this material became the case study for the *Lecture on serpent ritual*, in which he reflects on the 'basic elements of cosmological imagery' and the masked dance 'with live serpents' (Warburg, 1939: 272).

Following a similar impulse to discover a non-European culture not cut off from its metaphysical and mythological tradition, Artaud travelled to Mexico in 1936. For a month, he stayed with the Tarahumara people in the mountains, taking part in the Peyote ceremony and later writing about it in the essay *The Peyote Dance*. With these parallels in mind, I argue that the *Atlas* and the spells by Artaud unfold a *Poetics of Relation*. For Glissant, a poetics of relation is such a poetics 'in which each and every identity is extended through a relationship with the Other' (1997: 11). The category of Otherness denotes the cultural Other but refers also to unknown or suppressed layers within one's own identity. In that sense, a diagrammatic poetics of relations underpinning Warburg's project and Artaud's visual work destabilizes cultural separations, illuminating the dynamic process of translation and exchange.

After the unsuccessful premiere of the play *Les Cenci* in May of 1935, Artaud renounced his theatre practice, preparing for the trip to Mexico. He was in search for a metaphysical culture in which 'science and poetry are a single and identical thing' (Artaud, 1988: 373). At the same time, this was the period when his interest in occult[30] practices and astrology became more prominent. As Paule Thévenine noted in the preface to the publication on Artaud's visual work, it was in 1937, a few months after he had returned from Mexico (November 1936) and shortly before he embarked on his journey to Ireland, that he began sending out letters with a triple sign: 'The symbol of the feminine sex – which is also that of the planet Venus – augmented with an oblique stroke at its summit, on top of two triangles with the point upward, an almost magical sign' (1998: 15).

The voyage to Ireland turned out to be a complete disaster.[31] After a month of traveling across the island, he returned to Dublin where he was arrested and commanded to leave the country on a ship going to La Havre. As soon as he docked at the harbour back in France, Artaud was confined at a psychiatric hospital. It would be the beginning of his continuous stay in various psychiatric institutions for the next nine years. The context of the failed success in staging his own plays, the trips to Mexico and Ireland, together with the enhanced interest in the occult and the

---

[30] In his study on alternative spiritual performance and the theatre of the occult revival, Edmund B. Lingan observes that 'many occultists esteemed theatre as a sacred art with the potential to spiritually transform human beings' (2014: 2). Although Artaud could also be envisaged as a protagonist of the occult revival, Lingan only briefly mentions him in the book.

[31] A detailed account of his mysterious journey to Ireland is the book *Artaud 1937 Apocalypse* by Stephen Barber, in which the author collected and translated letters Artaud sent to France during his stay. See Barber (2019).

worsening of his mental condition, delineate the biographical circumstances in which Artaud began to draw/write his overtly diagrammatic spells (Figure 6).

In a letter sent from Galway to André Breton, he inserted a magic spell accompanied by the following instruction: 'I am entrusting to you a Magic spell that I'm sending to Madame X (...) You are going to see, once you have examined the Magic Spell, that things are about to become serious and this time, I'm going to the very end of everything' (Artaud in Barber, 2019: 31). Whilst this spell was considered a bad one and aimed to hurt 'Madame X' (Lise Deharme) because, as he wrote, she denied the existence of gods, the spell sent a few days later to Jacqueline Breton, André Breton's wife, had a protective function.

Figure 6 Antonin Artaud, Sort *Sonia Mossé* (*Spell for Sonia Mossé*), 1939, reproduced with the permission of Bibliothéque nationale de France

Deharme's spell is a diagrammatic arrangement of symbols, numbers and letters. In addition to the graphic operations, Artaud burned a hole in the middle part of the paper with a cigarette. This he will frequently do in many other letters and spells. In the short text in which he threatens her to 'perform some bad acting over your dead body' and thus prove that gods still exist, the page is decorated with four small triangles. The symbol of the planet Venus (♀) is repeated three times. Below the date (5. September 1937) in the upper-right corner, Artaud wrote the numbers 5, 9 and 2 in the first row, 14 and 2 in the second, and finally, the number 7 in the third row. At a distance from this cluster of numbers, he again placed the number 7.

In the spell addressed to Jacqueline Breton, the surface is left intact (without burns or perforations). In the first letter, the numbers are clustered into a triangular form with the top of the triangle being positioned downwards. In the second spell, the date (17th of September) is written in one line. A similar operation of addition is only performed with regard to the year: instead of writing the year '1937', Artaud wrote the number '2'. The text of the letter/spell reads:

> I will send a Magic Spell to the First One who dares to touch you. I am going to beat his little gob of a fake proud cock to a pulp. I am going to flay his arise in front of 100,000 people! HIS PAINTING WHICH WAS NEVER VERY STRIKING HAS NOW BECOME DEFINITIVELY
> BAD HIS VOICE IS TOO UGLY
> IT'S THE ANTICHRIST.
>
> (Artaud in Barber, 2019: 61)

The operation of adding numbers relates to a technique called Gematria, which consists of assigning numerical values to letters and expressing words as numbers. According to the German-Israeli philosopher and historian of religion Gershom Scholem, Gematria is of particular importance as one of the 'Cabbalistic methods of exegesis' (1954: 135). That Artaud was referring to the Kabbalah can be reconstructed from the letter to Breton in which he inserted the spell. He writes: 'I am against the Jews only to the extent that they have renounced the Kabbalah – all of the Jews who have not renounced the Kabbalah are with me – but the others: No' (Artaud in Barber, 2019: 34).

Written before his voyage to Ireland, the short text titled *The New Revelation of Being* (*Les Nouvelles Révélations de l'Être* Fr. Orig.), which offers an apocalyptic hallucination on the total destruction of the world by dark forces, Artaud explains the numerical operation he will also deploy in the creation of the spells: 'But November is the eleventh month of the year. And if, by Kabbalistically reducing the Numbers, I separate the two ones of 11 and undertake to add them, I obtain 2, which according to the Kabbala is the number of Separation-Destruction' (1965: 93).

The two magic spells set up the stage for similar 'eccentric graphic incident(s)' he would pursue creating until 1939 when the last spell was made (Rowell, 2017: 11). In relation to the spells from Ireland, the ones Artaud devised during the year of 1939 are more colourful. A vivid example is the spell conceived in 1939 and addressed to translator and writer Émile-Jules Grillot de Givry, who, at that moment, was already dead for ten years.[32] In the text, Artaud writes that de Givry is a big fan of spells and other magic curiosities. He sends it to him because it brings a 'perilous conspiracy against all evil sorcerers, and it is not part of the collection of the museum of witches, magicians and alchemists' (Artaud in Thévenine, 1998: 260).

The spell is performed on a folded piece of paper. It has two bigger holes in the middle of each side and more than a dozen smaller ones distributed around the paper. The text and the violet ink drawings spread out on the surface partly covered with blue and yellow zones. The text is framed with scribbles, lines and symbols like the six-pointed hexagram (the Star of David), several crosses, triangular and circular structures. Partly burned but still visible are two words: 'Seraphiel' and 'Chauriel'. This denotes angelic entities that are conjured during magic ceremonies. The procedure of overwriting and layering visual and textual elements supports to draw an analogy with manuscripts from the Middle Ages and Antiquity.[33] Similar to the spells, they often have the form of a palimpsest, a surface on which several layers of text and images are superimposed.

After having examined these three spells and before continuing our analysis with a diagrammatic drawing from the 1940s, I will consider their corporeality and performativity. If it can be argued that the spells are 'imbued with corporeal presence', what is their relation to theatre (Murray, 2014: 74)? In search for a non-psychological form of theatre that could function like *animated hieroglyphs*, Artaud concentrated on a new physical language based on visual signs (rather than words) that would unfold as succession of ritualistic gestures. He demands: 'We must learn to be mystics again' (1988: 55). In that way, society can *retheatricalize* theatre, returning to its ritualistic function.

---

[32] Émile-Jules Grillot de Givry (1874-1929) was a French writer interested in the occult sciences like the Kabbalah and alchemy. It is interesting to note that it was Givry who had translated the works of Paracelsus, a controversial figure in sixteenth-century philosophy, alchemy medicine and the book *Monas Hieroglyphica* by John Dee.

[33] Examining the manuscript of the thirteenth-century Dominican Berthold of Nuremberg and focusing on the diagrams therein, American art historian Jeffrey Hamburger draws the conclusion that diagrams were central to the making of medieval art and that much 'of medieval art is diagrammatic to its core' (2020: 227).

Furthermore, the request to eliminate entertainment, for which he advocates in *The Theatre and Its Double*, is connected to the reactivation of 'the ceremonial quality of a religious rite' (1988: 221). This coincides with an affirmation of the plastic and metaphysical beauty of absolute gestures. Situated between magic symbols and physicality, the spells render visible the interval between spirit and matter, revealing the transformation of theatre into a ritual practice. As Ros Murray argues, 'the spells are affective, seeking to transform the world around them, existing between bodies rather than replacing or representing a body' (2014: 84). At the same time, Artaud's requirement for the performance to have a direct and immediate effect on the body and skin of the audience shows the proximity to the haptic agency and efficacy of the spell.[34]

Invoking Spinoza 'who defined the body in terms of affects and who understood the body as a set of velocities, intensities and capacities of affecting and being affected', we could say that this definition offers a precise conceptual framework to comprehend the corporeality of the spells (Lepecki, 2006: 125). By breaking it down to the surface of the burned paper, Artaud pushes the body to the limits. It gets converted into a haptic texture crossed by forces of life and death. Opposing the mechanistic and dualistic concept of corporeality, Artaud affirms an image of the body that is connected to the mind and the cosmos through the metaphysics of breath.

Deciphering Artaud's concept of *affective athleticism*, Tony Gardner demonstrates how 'under the influence of the acupuncture needles, Artaud's long-standing interest in esotericsm and non-western metaphysics finds a new focus' (2003: 110). However, during the imprisonment period at the Rodez psychiatric clinic, Artaud was treated with electroshocks. As Gardner argues, the outcome of this painful therapy was the breakdown of the corporeal schema, which 'had its origins in a mechanistic world view through which the social bodies constructed by medicine and science are subjected to the same physical operations as machines or automatons' (2003: 115).

Being an expression of the psycho-social collapse and the violence of the medical apparatus, the diagrams cross the border between painting and drawing and act as symptoms of the fragmented body disconnected from life by the brutal machine of psychiatric power. In addition, these 'written drawings'[35] are coordinates of a virtual map Artaud designs to 'search for a body' (Derrida, 1998: 92). In the essay on the *Subjectile*, Derrida shows how the *theatrical hieroglyphics* and the pictograms of the spells render visible 'the magical force

---

[34] Exploring ritual practices and magic in Late Antiquity, Naomi Janowitz argues that 'magic was believed to be effective' (2002: 3).

[35] According to Thévenine, 'this unique quality in his work is just such a total confusion between the drawing and the writing, just such an impossibility of separating them' (1998: 40).

of writing sometimes ascribed to a proto-writing upon which we project all the myths of origin' (1998: 78).

Along this line of reasoning, one thing is indicative: Warburg and Artaud share a similar destiny regarding the symptom. The concept of the symptom seeks to grasp 'what we may call *the phantasmatic time of survival*' that is at the hearth of Warburg's notion of the pathos formula (Didi-Huberman, 2017: 28). Didi-Huberman identifies it first in the journals Warburg made during his stay at the psychiatric clinic in Kreuzlingen after the First World War. (2017: 244) In the case of Artaud's spells and letters, one experiences a similar *schizography*.

The desire to arrive at a visceral form of expression in which the signifier is not separated from the material world led Artaud to turn to medieval, pre-modern and non-Western esoteric traditions such as alchemy, the Kabbalah and Hinduism. Artaud notes that

> these are gestures, a word, a grammar, an arithmetic, a whole Kabbala and which shits at the other, which shits on the other, / no drawing made on paper is a drawing, the reintegration of a sensitivity misled, it is a machine that breathes, / this was first a machine that also breathes. (Artaud in Thévenine, 1998: 41)

The explicit corporeality comes also to the fore in the series of drawings he made during the last four years of his life (1944–1948). One example which will allow to deeper examine the *diagrammatic anatomy* of tormented flesh is the drawing entitled *Theatre of Cruelty (Le théâtre de la cruauté* Fr. Orig.) from 1946 (Figure 7).

The scene shows four bodies. Three of them are depicted in the coffins. The centre of the image occupies a red coffin with ornamentation in the form of blue lines and orange shapes resembling the contours of the Jewish alphabet. The coffin is open on the upper side. There, Artaud placed a dark figure with wild hair, wide open eyes and smudged face. On the right side, in the picture plane behind the coffin, we see a figure with male attributes. On the left, a female-looking figure appears with a more detailed anatomy of breasts, umbilicus and arms. Other creatures, whose forms are elusive and mysterious, are one headless figure with stretched legs resembling a cat (right below the central coffin). Next to it, a strange shape with identifiable legs and upper body but without a head. Framing the image with the text, Artaud scribbled 'Theatre of Cruelty'.

In his second manifesto of *The Theatre of Cruelty*, Artaud notes that he chooses the themes corresponding to the agitation and unrest of our times. These might appear directly in the gestures depicted 'according to the pictures in the most venerable holy books or ancient cosmogonies', like those Mexican, Hindu, Judaic and Iranian cosmogonies (Artaud, 1999: 95). Returning to magic and 'ancient hieroglyphs', the consequence is a visual narrative based on *affective sensuality* and the primacy of decentred spatiality (Artaud, 1999: 96).

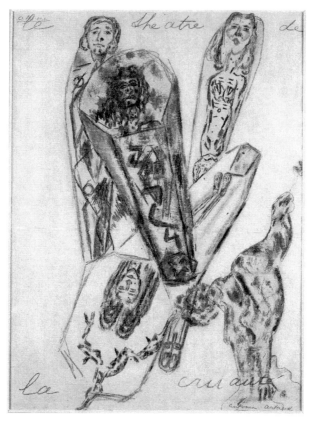

Figure 7 Antonin Artaud, *Le théâtre de la cruauté* (*Theatre of cruelty*), 1946,
reproduced with the permission of CNAC-MNAM Philippe Migeat

Such a practice comes into being through a combination of lines, forms, colours
and objects. Artaud designates it as the 'poetry of space', which he links to the
concept of the 'metaphysics in action'. As he writes: 'This whole active, poetic
way of visualizing stage expression leads us to turn away from present-day
theatre's human, psychological meaning and to rediscover a religious, mystical
meaning our theatre has forgotten' (1999: 32). With regard to the poetics of
performance diagrams, Artaud's attempt to return to a metaphysical and, thus,
magical conception of theatre, unfolds along a diagrammatic trajectory. It breaks
through the dualism of representation and the separation of the signifier and the
object, arriving at a zone of hybrid and intermedial intertwining. The spells, letters
and the drawings, I argue, are diagrams mapping the chaos of poetic creation and
translating Artaud's irrational visions into a disfigured anatomy of broken bodies
and haunted flesh pushed out of the equilibrium.

Interpreting the spells and the drawing through the optics of the Deleuzian[36] concept of the diagram, we could expand our thoughts on the diagrammatic agency of Artaud's *poetics of cruelty*. For Deleuze, the diagram designates an analogical flux that surpasses the regime of representation, resulting in the liberation of the body, the planes and the colour. More precisely, the liberation concerns the 'rupture with figurative resemblance' and it 'can occur only by passing through the catastrophe: that is through the diagram and its involuntary irruption' (2007: 83). Applied to the drawing from 1946 – which comes into being as a result (and symptom) of Artaud's personal catastrophe – we see the diagrammatic force working at the level of undoing figuration and acting precisely 'as an agent of transformation' (Deleuze, 2007: 109).

In relation to the paintings of Francis Bacon and Paul Cézanne, Deleuze affirms the diagram to comprehend the collapse of figuration and representation. Contrasting the analogical and the digital, he further associates it with the analogical language of relations, sensations and intensities, consisting of expressive/affective movement and paralinguistic signs. In addition, he refers to 'Artaud's theatre elevated scream-breaths' as a type of analogical language (2007: 79).

Another feature of the diagram is that it is made for something to emerge. Thus, it is a poetic tool par excellence. If applied to the context of Artaud's struggle to crystallize and distil precise metaphysical gestures – one that would move theatre and aesthetics away from psychological naturalism and representation – the concept of the diagram bestows an analytical framework for mapping these poetic and metaphysical transformations.

In an additional note on the Balinese theatre not included in the final version of *Theatre and His Double,* Artaud observes: 'Pure Production Theatre, mystic, religious idea, these men reduced to a *diagrammatic state* (italics by A.M), their gestures fall so precisely; that woody, drum music, reminds us of those robots made of hollow wood' (1999: 175). Due to their asymmetrical robes (costumes), the actors/dancers of the Balinese theatre whose performance he saw in 1927, looked (to him) like 'moving hieroglyphs'. As he further observes, these three-dimensional hieroglyphics are embellished with a certain number of gestures, 'strange signs matching some dark prodigious reality we have repressed once and for all here in the West' (1999: 44).

In her essay on the hieroglyphic body in Artaud, which she interprets as an expression of anti-rational metaphysics, Elizabeth Heard contends

---

[36] Artaud's carnal writing inspired Deleuze and Guattari to theorize the concept of the *Body without Organs* as 'field of immanence of desire' (2004: 170). However, while Deleuze and Guattari discuss the BwO in relation to questions of territoriality and cartography, there is no explicit reflection about its diagrammatic texture.

that it generates meaning dialectically: 'Through the tension of these oppositions' (2006: 41). For Artaud, hieroglyphics set in motion a spatial geometry that is sacred and visceral at the same time. Moreover, hieroglyphics signify the point in which mathematics converges with magic and metaphysics.

In one of the last written records that was entitled *50 Drawings to Murder Magic* (*50 dessins pour assassiner le magie*, Fr. Orig.) from 1948, Artaud wrote: 'These drawings are not the representation of figuration of an object of a state of mind of mind and heart, of an element or an event of a psychological kind, they are purely and simply the reproduction on the paper of a magical action that I have performed in true space' (Artaud, 2016: 16). In the preface to this short essay, Évelyne Grossman notes that this writing and drawing offer 'a non-focused scenography', on which the image-text transforms into a live actor (Grossman, 2016: XIII). In turn, the task of the 'actor' is to exorcize the demons.

Accordingly, the diagrammatic dimension of Artaud's poetics suggests the aesthetic condition in which the metaphysical sign acquires a haptic, carnal and material form.[37] Traversing the duality of the signifier and the object, as well as the opposition between nature and culture, performance diagrams proliferate a poetics embedded in magic and the ritual.

Conclusion

The *diagrammatic poetics* of Warburg and Artaud overlaps in the dynamic circulation of affects between text and image. In relation to the hieroglyphic body and drawing a parallel with the montage of Eisenstein, Heard comes to the conclusion that Artaud's practice of pictographic writing, together with his interest in the Kabbalah, 'reveals a concern with meaning and power manifest in the *material* objects that are letters and numbers' (2006: 43). In Warburg's case, the *Atlas* organizes images into series that have no final arrangement but can be shifted and reedited. One such visual material organized around permutation is the panel 50-51 where Warburg assembled images of the so-called Tarot[38] of Marseilles (Figure 8).

Comparing the mediality of the *Atlas* and the spells/drawing, we see that they intersect in the diagrammatic juxtaposition of images with words. In both cases, it materializes in the form of a *diagrammatic thought*, in which medial borders

---

[37] Deleuze insists that the diagram visually surpasses the duality of the optical and the tactile, giving birth to a haptic function (2007: 113).

[38] During the 1930s, we see in Artaud's work a growing interest in Gnosticism that can be linked to his 'increasing immersion in areas such as alchemy, the Cabbala, astrology and the Tarot' (Matheson, 2018: 141).

Figure 8 Aby Warburg, *Bilderatlas Mnemosyne*, 1927–1929, Panel 50–51.
London, Warburg Institute Archive

dissolve to give space to ambiguities and liminality.[39] Following the idea to transform the *iconic turn* into a *diagrammatic turn,* as Steffen Bogen and Felix Thürlemann suggest, we could argue that diagrams move across the opposition of text and image. Bogen and Thürlemann also write that diagrams are

---

[39] Analysing the memory and metaphors in the *Atlas,* Johnson demonstrates that it unleashes a diagrammatic thinking which 'trumps discursive language in its ability to furnish a single syncretic intuition' (2012: 59).

'semiotic objects with a quasi-magical character', which is something that becomes evident in Warburg and Artaud (2003: 22). The performance diagrams we have encountered and considered in this section proliferate connections between images, bodies and texts, unfolding an affective and *poetic cartography* whose coordinates are in a permanent motion.

3 Towards Sociopolitical Diagrams

In the two previous sections, the aim was to reconstruct the *cosmopoetical* dimension of performance diagrams in Vitruvius, Marlowe, Warburg and Artaud. The succeeding section concerns the *cosmopolitical diagram* in the performance *Paradise Now* (the Living Theatre, 1968) and the choreography *I Am 1984* (2008) by Barbara Matijević. Whereas the previous examples delineate the historical trajectory of performance diagrams, articulating various connections between theatre, epistemic operations and magical/ritualistic practices, the diagrams I will examine below disclose the contested aesthetic relationship between performance, activism and politics. Furthermore, in relation to the *I Am 1984* performance, I will survey the diagrammatic elements of choreographic notations. This I will do by asking how diagrams can contribute to rethinking the dualism between writing/drawing, practices of notation and dancing.

From a methodological viewpoint, this section deploys performance analysis to examine how diagrams are embodied and performed on stage. This will entail to reflect on the relationship between the diagrammatic script and its translation into the scenic event. As I have argued, 'before getting on stage, into the gallery, or elsewhere, many artists, choreographers, dramaturgs, scenographers and directors shape and diagrammatically prefigure their ideas' (2022: 1). Thus, the practice of diagramming performance figures as an epistemic instrument and as a poetic tool for theatre- and dance-making.

The intention is to demonstrate the potentiality of diagrams to enact non-representational models of performance-making. The first example (*Paradise Now*) sheds light on the *afterlife* of esoteric symbols that we have encountered in the spells, drawings and writings of Artaud. I am arguing that the Living Theatre developed a similar diagrammatic scheme that draws its inspiration from rituals, non-Western religious and esoteric traditions. The return to ancient myths, the mysterious language and signs of the Kabbalah, Tantric diagrams and the symbols of the Chinese *Book of Changes* (Ji-Ching) sets the framework to examine in more detail the relation between cosmopoetics and politics.

Drawing on Deleuze's concept of the diagram 'as a cartography that is coextensive with the whole social field', it is possible to comprehend the networks of forces that are fundamental to the organization of society (1988: 34). The concept of the diagram as a display of power relations leads Deleuze to conclude that 'every society has its diagram(s)' (34). Applying this statement to the two performances, I will assess the specific (inter)sociality of the diagram. If it can be contended that power (according to Deleuze) is diagrammatic, how and what kind of power is redistributed and negotiated in and through performance? Can performance diagrams reveal the nodes between society and art? Is it, in other words, possible and plausible to diagrammatically articulate the relationship between politics and aesthetics?

3.1 Diagrams of Revolutionary Bodies

Founded in 1947 by the poet Judith Malina and the painter, actor and director Julian Beck, the Living Theatre belongs to the tradition of avant-garde and experimental theatre influenced by the aesthetics of Bertolt Brecht, Erwin Piscator, Antonin Artaud and surrealist authors like Jean Cocteau or André Breton. Parallel to these influences, the Living Theatre grew out of a specific cultural context marked by the advent of abstract expressionism represented by artists such as Jackson Pollock, Willem de Kooning and Robert Rauschenberg. Apart from the aesthetic impulses, Malina and Beck drew their inspiration from the Kabbalah, the alchemical and gnostic tradition, Hinduism, Chinese divination texts and the literature on anarchism.[40] As an experimental and *bottom-up* practice, the Living Theatre employed 'techniques for de-subjectifying performance, including not only collective creation but also improvisation and the use of chance procedures' (Cull, 2013: 23).

After the first decade in which the group staged plays such as Gertrude Stein's *Doctor Faustus Lights the Light*, Alfred Jarry's *Ubu Roi*, T.S. Eliot's *Sweeney Agonistes*, Strindberg's *Ghost Sonata* and Cocteau's *Orpheus*, the success came with Jack Gelber's play *The Connection* (1959) and, finally, with the production of *Paradise Now* (1968). As one theatre critic had noted in 1962, 'Chance, accident, the refusal to formulate things too precisely, the insistence on maintaining some semblance of the "chaos" of the world is a thread which runs through all the productions of the Living Theatre, and is at one the source of its excitement and danger' (Mee, 1962: 202).

---

[40] Beck points out the alchemical dimension of *Paradise Now* and writes: 'Paradise Now: the search for alchemical formulae: in addition to incantation: scientific procedure: dialectic (...) What magic, what alchemical changes, unexpected, unknown as yet to man, can produce a state of freedom in a society in which it is not possible for one of us to be free until we are all free?' (Beck, 1972: n.p.).

While the performance has already been examined by numerous scholars, the diagram handed out to the audience as a poster and booklet did not receive any significant attention. In the words of Judith Malina:

> The program was a poster-size map, showing Ten Rungs, leading upward from The Rite of Guerrilla Theatre, outside the gates of Paradise, to the highest vision of the permanent revolution. Each rung consisted of a Rite, and a Vision and a Political Action in which the audience took part, or even invented. What looked like chaos was in fact a free-flowing movement toward more and more elevated forms. (2012: 181)

In the form of a classification table, the diagram displays three distinct columns, two of which show the contours of two human bodies (Figure 9). On the left side, we see a naked male figure depicted frontally and facing the viewer. On the right, a female figure. She is also naked and occupies the same position as her male counterpart. In the middle part, there are numerous squares with hand-written texts. Below the feet of the man, the text reads: 'This chart is the map of the Living Theatre.' In the middle part: 'The essential trip is the voyage from the one to the many Paradise Now,' and on the lower left part: 'The plot is the Revolution Collective Creation.' The two bodies and the middle part are divided into rectangular zones filled either with text or signs.

On the left side, the figure is placed within a rectangular grid that divides it into eight parts, plus one part above the head. In addition, on the edge to the right side, the eight fields are divided into three parts, so that the totality of the cells is forty-eight. Every rectangular cell contains handwritten words and phrases (twenty-four in total) like: 'Modesty', 'Abundance Fullness', 'Conflict', 'Peace', 'Return the Turning point', The creative', 'Enthusiasm' and 'Progress'. Next to the these words are twenty-four Ji-Ching hexagrams, each made out of six horizontal lines that are either sold (Yang) or broken (Yin).

On the right side, the space of the diagram is organized in a similar way with a division into eight rectangular parts. Inside the boxes on the left side, we can see circles with words like: 'Stasis', 'Illusion', 'Fear', 'Rigidity', 'Alienation-Inhibition', 'Ignorance', 'Hostility resulting from an unsatisfactory life' and 'The Culture'. Above and below the circles, there are words with three arrows pointing to the next circle. We read: 'Impetus', 'Creative energy', 'Energetic action', 'Movement', 'Love Force', 'Enthusiasm', 'Truth force' and 'Aesthetic assault'.

In the column next to it are also eight cells with eight sentences. The first top box reads: 'The Rung of God and Man', the lower one: 'The Rung of good and Evil'. On the left side of the female figure, each zone of the body is paired with a colour; white on the top and black on the bottom. Hence, being presented as framed by words and symbols, the two bodies are depicted in correspondence with the esoteric systems and signs of the Kabbalah, Ji-Ching and Tantric Yoga.

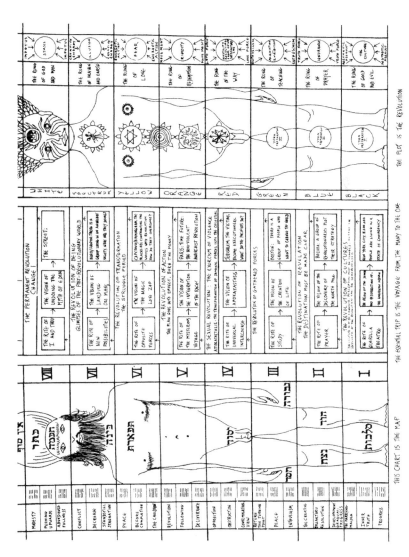

Figure 9 The Living Theatre, diagram of the performance *Paradise Now*, 1968, reproduced with the permission of the Living Theatre Estate

The middle part consists of eight rows that are additionally divided by three rows and, in the middle row, another three boxes related with arrows. This part of the diagram contains much more text and has no additional symbols or images. On the top, we read: 'The permanent revolution change' and on the bottom: 'The Revolution of Cultures. Culture must be changed. Perception must be changed. So that the Usefulness of the Revolution can be Comprehended.'

The eight boxes in the middle part denote different rites such as: 'The Rite of I and Thou', 'The Rite of Opposite Forces', 'The Rite of Prayer' and 'The Rite of Guerilla Theatre'. With arrows, these boxes are related with the next boxes. The sentences revolve around the classification of visions: 'The Vision of Undoing the Myth of Eden', 'The Vision of the Integration of Races', 'The Vision of Apokatastasis'.[41] Finally, the third group of boxes (on the right) are geographical signifiers such as 'Hanoi/Saigon', 'Capetown/Birmingham', 'Paris' and 'Bolivia'.

The male figure is inscribed with letters of the Hebrew alphabet distributed across the different body parts. This particular diagram mirrors the kabbalistic *Tree of Life*. It is made of ten Sephiroth symbolizing the divine emanations through which the creative force of divinity manifests in the visible world. As Scholem shows, the Sephiroth unveil the hidden world of divine creation and, together with the twenty-two letters of the (Hebrew) alphabet, form the *Tree of life*. They illuminate stages of the inner world through which god descends into the material realm, gaining visibility in the shape of a tree. In short, the Sephiroth constitute the diagram of the cosmos.

In contrast to the *Tree of Knowledge* which, according to the Kabbalah, can be identified with the oral Tora, the *Tree of Life* is equated 'with the written Tora' (Scholem, 1969: 68). Furthermore, the *Tree of Life* expresses the myth of cosmogony, which begins with emanation from the realm of the boundless light (*Ein-Sof*). This word, written in Hebrew letters (אֵין סוֹף), appears on the top of the male figure, giving us a clear indication that the *Paradise Now* diagram incorporates the symbolism and language of the Kabbalah.

However, the diagram of the *Tree of Life* is not presented in its usual form with the ten points and the twenty-two paths (in the form of straight lines) connecting them. Instead, the male figure depicts the symbolic image of the primordial man called *Adam Kadmon*. Reflecting on the kabbalistic significance of this figure, Scholem writes:

> The simile of the man is as often used as that of the tree. The Biblical word
> that man was created in the image of God means two things to the Kabbalist:

---

[41] The Greek term *Apokatasasis* (ἀποκατάστασις Gr. Orig.) is a theological and eschatological concept borrowed from Orthodox Christianity. It refers to the restoration of the primordial unity between man and God, which had existed before mankind indulged in sinful activities.

first, that the power of the Sephiroth, the paradigm of divine life, exists and is active also in men. Secondly, that the world of the Sephiroth, that is to say the world of God the Creator, is capable of being visualized under the image man the created. (1954: 215)

The limbs of the human body are images of a spiritual mode of existence, and it shows the figure of Adam Kadmon (Figure 10). The conception of god as an organism and the idea that Sephiroth are limbs of the mystical man illuminates the meaning of the anatomical symbolism mirrored with the diagram. The myth

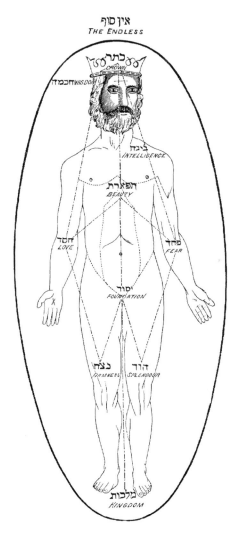

Figure 10 Adam Kadmon, diagram illustrating the Tree of Life, From Christian Ginsburg, *The Kabbalah – its Doctrines, Development & Literature*, 1865. Wikimedia Commons

of creation personified in Adam Kadmon is closely connected to the idea of 'the decisive crisis of all divine and created being' (Scholem, 1969: 112). In the Kabbalah, it is narrated through the allegory of the broken vessels. According to Scholem, the central image is that of the dying primordial king, whose death is the consequence of the broken of harmony that existed between masculine and feminine elements.

Drawing on idea of the mystical body and the cosmological/ontological crisis, we might ask, how does it relate to the performative practice of the Living Theatre? Writing about the body in contemporary society, Julian Beck observes: 'The lost body rediscovered. The body numbed by the industrial society. The body clamped shut by capitalistic morality, the body screwed by poverty. The body liberated by the food and poetry of revolutions. The body alive in action' (1972: n.p.). In his aesthetic vision, the body has a sacred status and has to be liberated from the oppression of capitalism and societal violence. Echoing Artaud, Beck argues for a 'Theatre of the Body That Not Only Sees' but has the capacity to induce the flow of desire (1972: n.p.). That body, in turn, can revolutionize, thus undo the alienated libidinal economies of capitalist society.

Differentiating between the conservative and the revolutionary aspects of Jewish mysticism expressed in the Kabbalah, Scholem notes that the conservative mystics obey the religious authority of tradition. The revolutionary mystic, on the other hand, challenges authority. As he writes, with the second type 'we have the revolutionary aspect of mysticism in its purest form' (1969: 11). Finally, as the most radical and subversive manifestation of mysticism, Scholem evokes the figure of 'nihilistic mysticism', one that is suppressed and prosecuted by religious authorities. If it can be argued that the Living Theatre embodies this revolutionary and nihilistic type of mysticism, it sheds light on the relationality between mystical practices and anarchism. They intersect in *Paradise Now*. In other words, what the revolutionary mystic studying the Torah and the anarchistic theatre collective have in common is a yearning to restore the harmony between the cosmos, the body and society.

The female figure standing on the right side is adorned with numerous geometrical patterns. Circular in form, these shapes create a vertical structure running across the middle of the body from the forehead to the ankles. The lowest three carry the inscription 'Yoga Preparation I-III'. The other six circles are flower-like patterns with a hexagram, an accumulation of arrows, concentric circles and a shape resembling an insect in the middle. In the Hindu tradition, these symbols are called *Yantras*. Their function is to enable, activate and control the expansion of psychic forces during meditation.

According to Indian religious scholar Madhu Khanna, the Yantra is a geometrical diagram and presents a vital 'part of the esoteric discipline of

Indian tradition' (1994: 7). These abstract symbols can be retraced back to early Indian History (3000 BC). Among the numerous artefacts from the Bronze Age, archaeologists have unearthed coins and seals marked with geometrical figures, crosses and squares. The concept of the Yantra (as it is developed within Tantrism) is a ritual-oriented system that grew out of the Hindu religion during the eighth century AD.

It is believed that the Yantra is the sacred dwelling of deities, acting as a revelatory 'symbol of cosmic truth' (Khanna, 1994: 12). Symbolizing the unity of man with the universe, the Yantra is a ritualistic instrument to achieve harmony between the macrocosm and the microcosm. Its immanent diagrammatic structure translates 'psychic realities into cosmic terms and the cosmos into psychic planes' (Khanna, 1994: 22). In the Vedic and Tantric tradition, the flower-like circles are also known as Lotuses or Chakras. These are significant energetic meridians traversing the body, and they can be activated during meditation and ritual ceremonies. Writing about the cultural/mythological relevance of flowers and their hidden geometry, Keith Critchlow observes that in the Vedic religious context 'flowers were treated as part of the continuum from the physical to the metaphysical. For example, the subtle *chakras* of the body are visualized as flowers (often called lotuses) and indicate human spiritual development in this tradition' (2011a: 62).

The geometrical patterns of flowers, as Critchlow illustrates with the diagrams in his book, correspond to the 'flower-like time-traces', the trajectories each visible planet sets in motion during its rotation around the sun (2011a: 76). In other words, through the system of correspondences, the rhythmic pattern of planetary movements (macrocosm) can be related to the shapes of flowers on the earth (microcosm).[42] The concept and practice of Tantric Yoga depicted with the diagram provide a tool to liberate libidinal energies and to increase the 'consciousness of the physical apparatus', overcoming 'the results of the psycho-physical repression' (Beck, 1972: n.p.). Central to the sacred teaching of Tantrism is a holistic apprehension of the body not separated but in connection with the cosmic energies. It must be also noted that the Tantric Renaissance (700–1300 AD) entailed a re-evaluation of the feminine principle, which resulted in it becoming a 'total symbol of divine power (...) an emblem of kinetic or potential energy' (Khanna, 1994: 54).

As we can see, the performance chart of *Paradise Now* operates within a diagrammatic regime that constellates and multiplies cultural and esoteric symbols. The polarity between the male and the female mirrors the division

---

[42] As Kanna shows, being a potent and dynamic sacred symbol, Yantras are also employed in astrology and ritual worship. See Kanna (1994: 23).

between the 'East' and the 'West' and between the different ritualistic systems whose merging becomes necessary for the revolutionary action. The 'beautiful non violent anarchist revolution' (Beck, 1972: n.p.) of *Paradise Now* pushes bodies into a liminal experience. According to Beck and Malina, this *theatre of emergency* and total experience is achieved by the physical participation of the spectator. The result is the abolition of the separation between the performer and the spectator. Hence, as a map charting the dramaturgical trajectories of *Paradise Now*, the diagram blends poetic with political action. In doing so, it is subversive to the polarity and tensions between the 'East' and the 'West'.

Discussing the first period (late 1940s–1964) of Becks and Malina's work, art critic Allan Antliff reconstructs how the development of poetic theatre paired with pacifist-anarchist activism made visible the contradictions between the politics and the theatrical work. He asserts that Beck and Malina 'enacted a politics of 'ardor' intent on triggering affective responses amongst the general populace' (2015: 8). The aim was to fight institutional oppression and violence. A decisive moment in the development of the Living Theatre's aesthetics happened during the rehearsals of Jack Gelber's play *The Connection* (1959). This was when Malina and Beck were introduced to Artaud's *The Theatre and Its Double*. Scenes in which drug addicts inject real heroin on stage brought down the imaginary *fourth wall*, radicalizing theatre on the level of affectivity.[43] As Antliff further observes, this made the performance synonymous with the poetic value of the *theatre of cruelty* 'that could bring us face-to-face with our deep seated destructive impulse' (2015: 19).

At the moment of *Paradise Now*'s creation, the Living Theatre was an artistic collective consisting of thirty-four artists and nine kids. As it can be reconstructed from the *Paradise Now: Notes* (1969), the discussions concerning the structure and aim of the performance began in January 1968 while the collective was staying in Sicily. In one of the first notes, we read that the performance should provide 'glimpses of the post-revolutionary road' because: 'Paradise Now is How to Get There' (Beck in The Living Theatre, 1969: 91). To this, Malina replies: 'We can't map out how to get there because we don't have the map. But we have to make a map. This is the paradox' (Malina in The Living Theatre: 91). The *cartographic impulse* expressed here can be understood as an equivalent of the diagrammatic journey that is not only implicated with the chart but becomes the explicit dramaturgical axis of the performance. In other words, *Paradise now* is an attempt to map and, at the same time, perform the map to paradise.

---

[43] In an interesting observation about the role of psychedelic drugs in the creation of *Paradise Now*, James Penner shows how their usage inspires 'the actor/performer to reject the traditional barriers (the fourth wall) and to participate in a more inclusive and less structured performance/creative event' (2014: 78).

The twenty-four boxes in the middle pillar, starting with the 'The Rite of the Guerilla Theatre' (on the lower left part) and finishing with the box 'Street' (top right), mark the dramaturgical trajectory of the performance. Together with the eight stages of the revolution and the eight rungs depicted in the boxes on the left frame, the diagram navigates into 'a vertical ascent towards nonviolent revolution' (Penner, 2014: 81). As the journalist Erika Billeter writes, Julian Beck collected all the suggestions the group members shared during the rehearsal process and designed the diagram for the show. It became the 'basis of the performance' (Billeter, 1968: 101).

Without having a dramatic text as a script, *Paradise Now* was staged as a series of tableau vivants with bodies transformed into images and sculptural compositions. Besides the living images created through various corporeal relations, the performers were chanting and reciting sentences like: 'You are not allowed to travel without a passport', 'I don't know how to stop the war', 'You can't live if you don't have money', 'I am not allowed to smoke marihuana', 'I am not allowed to take my clothes off' and 'How much did you pay to get in here?' These utterances aimed at critically questioning the social norms and taboos that constitute the status quo of society. Consequently, such a performative procedure abolished the traditional division between performer/audience, resulting in a less structured event relying on chance and improvisation.

One element of the scenic action which seems worth focusing on a bit closer is the composition of letters with the naked bodies. Composing words like 'Anarchism' and 'Paradise' that are embodied in front of the audience, the Living Theatre creates a situation in which the performance becomes a space of corporeal writing and reading (Figure 11). In that way, *Paradise Now* progresses as a translation of the diagram from the two-dimensional page to the three-dimensional stage. In other words, the diagrammatic mechanism of *Paradise*

Figure 11 The Living Theatre, photo of the performance *Paradise Now*, 1968, reproduced with the permission of the Living Theatre Estate

Now becomes evident not only in the poster/booklet but is as an important element of performance-making.

In his study on the correlation between dancing and writing, German dance scholar and theologian Alexander H. Schwan takes up Mallarmé's notion of *écriture corporelle* (corporeal writing) and shows how dance movements intertwine the act of writing with the written trace. Among the different case studies, such as the works of Trisha Brown, Jan Fabre and William Forsythe, he discusses the figure of the human alphabet which have the form of playfully anthropomorphized letters. One such example he refers to is the woodcut by Peter Flötner, *The Human Alphabet* (*Das Menschenalphabet* Ger. Orig.), from 1534.

In the image, we see naked human bodies arranged in such a way as to depict individual Latin letters from A to Z. The scene renders visible the visual feature of letters and in doing so confuses 'the borders between acrobatics, erotic and (. . .) dance movement' (Schwan, 2022: 72). In *Paradise Now*, the animated and choreographed letters resulting from the translation of the diagram into an embodied action bring to the fore a form of *corporeal writing* that subverts the dualism between words/images and is explicitly diagrammatic.

To conclude, the twofold diagram in *Paradise Now* develops as a trajectory of revolutionary action intending to cut across the fractures of ontological, spiritual and political divisions. This entails blending the 'exterior/anarchist/communist revolution' with 'the interior/spiritual/sexual revolution' (Beck, 1972: n.p.). As a constellation of forces, the performance diagram sets the stage for the 'voyage from the many to the one' (as it can be read at the bottom of the middle pillar). Regarding the different forces that were activated, Beck writes:

> In *Paradise Now* we called into action mysterious forces: the influence of color, the wisdom of the Book of Changes, the physical-spiritual journey of Kundalini, the arousal of the energy which rests in the chakras, the holy world vision of the Chassidim, the high vision of the Kabbala, we energized the body segment by segment, and we devised rituals, movements, sounds, visions, and cadences that carried the actors (the guides) and the public into trance. (1972: n.p.)

In its intention to confront capitalist alienation, the diagram appears intersocial and agitational. By aligning different functions of theatre with an activist agenda, it transforms the performance into an aesthetic practice that is 'both poetic and political' (Pellerin, 2018: 1). Finally, materializing the point in which the poetic, the political and the ritualistic lines interconnect, the diagram constitutes the *mise en scène* of revolution.

Offering a view on the sociopolitical trajectories of subjectivation, the diagram that I will analyse next is an example of how it serves to activate a performative narration revolving around the discursive construction of subjectivities. As André Lepecki argues in his book *Singularities: Dance in the Age of Performance*, one critical task of dance and performance studies is to reflect on those conditions of dancing and writing against 'the conditions of neoliberal conditioning' (2016: 5). While in 1968 when *Paradise Now* was performed, an utopian spirit circulated among various social and counter-cultural movements and there were high hopes for a revolutionary change, six decades later, no such revolutionary spirit seems to be present. In fact, the multiplication of crisis (ecological, ideological, economic) and the sophistication of surveillance technologies additionally limit any potential liberation capable of challenging the neoliberal paradigm and its dysfunctional, suicidal mechanism.

In the forty years (1968–2008) separating the creation of *Paradise Now* and the performance *I Am 1984*, the social and ideological structures have been radically transformed. Although the two performance diagrams I am analysing in this section occur in different cultural and historical contexts, my argument is that they can initiate a comparative and critical reflection about the intersections of performance, the political and the social. As Lepecki points out, the advent of 'performance' signifying a new aesthetic category usually identified with happenings, performance art, body art, actionism and post-modern dance' happened parallel 'with the transition between liberal capitalism and its neoliberal integrated global form' (2016: 8). In that sense, I discuss the two performance diagrams as expressions of the new condition of power that becomes co-extensive with the political and aesthetic practice.

3.2 Graphic Tools of Choreography

Within the spectrum of the performing arts, the discourses and practices of choreography show a special relation with diagrams and diagrammatic operations. Etymologically, the Greek compound 'choreography' – χορεία + γραφή (circular dance + writing) – makes the relation between movement and writing explicit, allowing us to expand the reflection on the graphic dimension and appearance of dance and performance. Analysing how visual and performative questions align with questions of trace, writing and inscription, Mark Franko illuminates the connections 'between the pictorial Figure and the dancing body' (2019: 98). In his view, dance pushes writing into the realm of visuality, transforming the notion of drawing into that of a drawing body. This furthermore implies that drawing is also scriptural and that dance, as a *movement-writing*, creates a non-linear scripture.[44]

---

[44] Recalling Deleuze's concept of the diagram, Franko argues that notations make movement repeatable and in doing so conserve the relationship between the body and the 'letter and/or the diagram' (2019: 100).

Historically, we could return to Thoinot Arbeau's *Orhesography* (1589) and Raoul Auger Feuillet's *Chorégraphie ou l'art de décrire la danse* (1700), both of which were conceived as systems of archiving ballroom and theatrical dances in the early modern period. Interweaving musical notation with images, figures and written texts, these two examples 'recorded a trajectory through space', pointing out the fact 'that the trace marks left behind might serve to reconstitute the dancer's movement' (Franko, 2019: 99–100). The non-linear 'movement-writing' of choreography reveals a transactional relation between dance and scripturality. Organizing and mediating the knowledge of movement necessary to perform the dance, it appears as a diagram. However, the notations of Arbeau and Feuillet do not only convey knowledge about the movement. They show an immanent poetic quality emerging from the aesthetic combination of visual and textual signs.

The reception of notations unfolds as a hybrid practice of reading, visual apprehension and imagination. Accordingly, the consequence is an intermedial constellation of iconic and scriptural forms that not only archive movement patterns but also become the source of performance-making. Operating as diagrams – in the sense that they act as tools to visualize and translate movement – notations oscillate between documentation and concept, thereby marking the 'relational position between the work and performance, between image/text and body/movement' (Brandstetter, Hoffman and Maar, 2010: 14). The focus on spatiality and relationality brings the *notation-as-diagram* conceptually close to the practice of mapping, particularly in the depiction of dance transformed into graphic and spatial patterns.

For Sybille Krämer, dance that 'emerges out of choreography' contains 'an immanent diagrammatic dimension' that gets activated when notations are enacted by the moving body (2016: 78). The implicit schema underlying the diagram reveals another feature of notations: reproducibility and iterability. As a medium that enables the repetition of performance and movement, notations proliferate alternative ways to rethink the dualism between the ephemerality of dance and the stability of the archive. Furthermore, they allow us to comprehend the processuality of performance. This implies that notations shed new light on the changing materiality, the various stages and contingencies of choreographic becoming. Instead of fixed meanings, *notations-as-diagrams* multiply and support polysemy and hybridity.

Differentiating between the choreographic regime of classical ballet and the contemporary, experimental dance, art historian Natilee Harren observes that the first establishes an 'iconic relationship' between the dance, the body per-forming the dance and the graphic representation of the dance. (2022: 148) Here, the ideal form of the dance is privileged above everything else.

In contrast, experimental dance has a tendency to align with a Deleuzian notion of the diagram, which implies that the immanent diagram of the individual's dancer's body may not be expected to fully assimilate to the dance. Harren's conclusion is that the power of the diagram lies in its virtuality. It 'appears rather as a set of properties and spatial relationships that are flexible and manipulable, a tool or guide for ushering forth the unpredictable and unfamiliar' (2022: 149).

According to French dance historian Laurence Louppe, who draws on Stéphen Mallarmé, dance evolves into a *counter-writing* which is the reverse of any grapheme, and, thus, it leads to the abolishment of the letter. As a trajectory between the real and the sign, dance resists to be fully absorbed into an icon or its index. And yet, as Louppe observes, 'the site of inscription (...) has always, almost fatally, been bound to the destiny of Western dance' (1994: 11). More than just a document and archival record of the moving body, graphic notations expose the visual and scriptural forces at work in choreographic creation.

While for Feuillet, the concept of choreography originally signified the practice to trace and write down movements, our contemporary understanding reduces it to the act of composing dance. As a consequence, notations and diagrams are rarely presented to the audience and remain anonymous and secret. On the other hand, marking 'a conjunctive tissue between the body, its movement, and the space of projection where the inner score can unfurl', notations nevertheless participate 'in a long scriptural history by which movement has sought to inscribe itself and to remain in memory' (Louppe, 1994: 16–17). Evoking a passage from the memoirs of the Russian ballet dancer Tamara Karasavina, Louppe recalls how for the ballerina, notations were 'cabalistic signs of black magic' (1994: 20). In light of these considerations, what can be said about graphic and diagrammatic residues of dance and their relation to the text?

In his deconstructive analysis of Mallarmé's short essay *Mimique*, Derrida emphasizes the process of spacing by which writing comes into being as an endless event of folding. The figure to which he keeps returning in his analysis is the figure of ballet and dance. Quoting Mallarmé's idea that dance is 'hiero-glyphic', Derrida illuminates how 'the hieroglyph, the sign, the cipher moves away from its "here and now"', and thus expose the space of deferral and displacement (1981: 241). Diagrammatic leftovers and notations of dance galvanize a scrambled scripture moving back and forth between indexes, graphs and undecipherable signs that resemble divination scripts of some forgotten and secret rituals. In turn, dance *dis-appears* as a corporeal writing haunted by the graphic phantoms, dwelling in the liminal zone between presence and absence.

To further consider the figure of writing in relation to dance is an invitation to ponder about the potentiality of the body to serve as an archiving tool.

According to Lepecki, *the body as archive* manifests in the 'will to archive' and as 'a capacity to identify in a past work still non-exhausted creative fields of 'impalpable possibilities'' (2016: 120). From the perspective of choreography, the archival impulse immanent to the body also reveals itself as a dynamic system of transformation, a critical point 'where virtuals and actuals exchange place' (2016: 127). If we can argue that performance diagrams unfold a comparable trajectory traversing the actual and the virtual, they can be deployed to reflect on the multiple temporalities of choreography and the creation of affective archives of movement.

One such example in which the diagram and diagramming are central to the narration and performance of memory is the choreography *I Am 1984* by Barbara Matijević and Giuseppe Chico.[45] The piece premiered in 2008, in Zagreb, and it performatively explores the year 1984. Different events, dates and persons diagrammatically connect to the autobiography of the performer (Matijević), who was born in 1978 in socialist Yugoslavia (nowadays Croatia). Having the format of a lecture performance, *I Am 1984* engages in a choreographed reconstruction of historical events that are not only narrated but also depicted and constellated with the help of graphs, lines and drawings.

It begins with Matijević entering the stage saying, 'Good evening' and turning on the music on her white computer. The scenography is reduced to a black wall with a large sheet of white paper[46] and the computer placed on a black plinth positioned next to the paper. After shortly leaving the stage, she re-enters carrying pens to draw/write the diagram. 'Faster, higher, stronger', says Matijević, and continues: 'It is with these words, spoken for the first time in Athens in 1896 that on the 20th of July 1984, the 23rd Summer Olympic Games were launched in Los Angeles.' Telling this, she starts drawing the diagram. She first marks a dot, writing the year '1984' and then draws a line to the left side of the paper. There, she will draw the five circles symbolizing the Olympic Games. In this part, Matijević also mentions that the indigenous Tongva people, who inhabited the L.A. area for thousands of years believed that 'telling stories at night made the stars move in the sky'.

The motif of the stars and the galaxy is brought up again just a few moments later when the performer writes the initials of the composer John Williams, who composed the soundtrack for the film *Star Wars* and the theme song to the series *Lost in Space*. His initials are further linked to the iconic helmet of Darth Wader and then to the contours of the Disney castle whose orchestra Williams was

---

[45] Matijević and Chico are an artistic duo and in 2007 they founded the theatre Company Premiere Stratageme based in Paris. In their projects, they explore the influences of digital culture and media on storytelling and are engaged in creating forms of auto-fictional performances. For a more detailed description, see www.premierstratageme.net/en/bio/.

[46] On other occasions the diagram was written directly on a black wall.

conducting. This fact of Williams conducting the big orchestra Matijević connects to her own initials ('B.M.'). At that time, she was six years old and took the oath as one of Tito's pioneers. 'B.M.', says Matijević: 'takes part in the collective choreography[47] together with other 140 Tito's pioneers, who composed different formations in the middle of the football stadium, notably the formation of the name 'Tito'. While B.M. and the youth on the parade were prevented from forming a star due to the heavy rain, on the field of the Olympic Games in Los Angeles: 'Hundreds of youngsters can form the words "Welcome" and "Regan"', says Matijević.

The performance continues with Matijević sharing her childish fantasy: she wanted to break into the television set (Figure 12). The year 1984, we find out in the lecture, was also the year when the personal computer Apple Macintosh was introduced by means of a television commercial aired during the Super Bowl event. In this part, Matijević teaches the audience that Steve Jobs and Bob Dylan had a spiritual figure in common: Timothy Leary. Best known for his slogan 'Tune in, Turn on, Drop out', Leary was the icon of the psychedelic

Figure 12 Premiere Stratagème, photo of the performance *I am 1984*, 2008, Barbara Matijević, photo by Cici Olsson, reproduced with the courtesy of the artist

---

[47] The so-called Day of Youth Parade was a spectacular manifestation held to commemorate the birthday of Yugoslav President Josip Broz Tito. Drawing on the research by Andrew Hewitt, it could be argued that the Youth Parade was a paradigmatic manifestation of a *social choreography* that enables us to comprehend the centrality of aesthetics and choreography to the production of social configurations (2005).

movement and also known for advocating the use of mind-altering substances like LSD. The year 1984 is significant for B.M. because she saw a ballet performance on television for the first time in her life. From that moment on, she dreamt of becoming a ballerina.

'That year,' she continues, 'Yugoslavia won its first golden medal at the Winter Olympic Games in Sarajevo.' In this context, she informs the audience that B.M. had found a book on ballet and that she was eagerly copying the movements in front of the mirror. In the middle part of the performance, Matijević tells the story of the famous Croatian and Yugoslav ballerina Mia Slavenska, who collaborated with the Walt Disney Studio on the movie *Fantasia*. Addressing the audience with the words: 'So, let's write down: a woman disappears,' Matijević deletes the initials of Slavenska that she wrote next to the red drawing of a ballet shoe.

Her narration further confers information on artists who had died on stage while performing (like Bela Lugosi) or the Butoh dancer Yoshiyuki Takada. After she finishes this story, she deletes their initials in the same manner as she did it with Slavenska. The next topic is about the science fiction writer Isaac Asimov, who thought that 'robots have the right to attack people if they put humanity into danger'. Further, we learn that Asimov introduced words like 'robotics' and 'psychohistory' into the English language and that one of the most famous robots from popular culture, *Hall 9000*, explains how 'nobody learned computers how to change over to the year 2000'.

While telling the story of the unavoidable economic catastrophe due to the millennial transition, at the bottom of the paper, Matijević writes numbers from 90 to 10. Her next story is about the virtual online platform *Second Life* created in 2003 as a multimedia, role-playing game. We learn that 1984 was also the year in which the spectacular performance by Marcus Allen during the Super Bowl XVIII took place. As Matijević says, it 'remains one of the most beautiful, magic and inexplicable moments in the whole history of the Super Bowl'. Attaining an absolute equilibrium, Allen ran 74 yards and Los Angeles Raiders won the game. Parallel to the narration of this significant achievement, she draws vertical green lines across the paper.

These are succeeded by red lines resembling the waves and graphs that appear in diagrammatic depictions of diverse phenomena such as weather oscillations, biological processes, thermal waves, stock market crashes, ranking criteria of the internet search engine or, as Matijević says, 'social phenomena such as panic, applause, shyness or stage fright' (Figure 13). All these phenomena, she concludes, are governed by the same impulse for absolute equilibrium. The last story is about the gamer Billy Mitchell. He was successful in reaching the perfect score in the video game Pac-Man. His example shows how the

Figure 13 Premiere Stratagème, photo of the performance *I am 1984*, 2008, Barbara Matijević, photo by Cici Olsson, reproduced with the courtesy of the artist

search for equilibrium is a necessary condition for top performance. To this end, Matijević emphasizes that Mitchell actually became Pac-Man by using a technique of visualization. The performance ends with David Bowie's song *Love you till Tuesday*.

Her voice, intonation, gestures and costume (red turtleneck sweater, green dress, white socks and red shoes) make her appear as a lecturer and school teacher. During the forty-five minutes of the piece, the focus is on the paper/surface representing a schoolroom blackboard. Apart from the writing, when Matijević turns her back to the audience, most of the time, the performance happens frontally, which enhances the flatness of the diagram. Using black, green and red pens to write and draw, she conceives the performance as a lecture that activates a diagrammatic and pedagogical space where drawings dynamically interfere with lines, words and numbers. At the same time, *I Am 1984* unfolds as a choreography disseminating and organizing historical information on key events in popular culture, media and sports, as well as autobiographical data into a relational assemblage. The piece operates in the framework known as lecture performance.

As an artistic concept situated on the threshold between academic lecture and performance, it was established in the early 1960s. Blurring the boundaries that separate scholarly forms of knowledge production and pedagogy from artistic practice, and art from life, lecture performance is often engaged in 'performing knowledge' (Rainer, 2017: 10). In the case of *I Am 1984*, the performance proliferates and embodies a space of knowledge, transforming it into an aesthetic practice.

Within the parameters of genre, the piece adopts a model of performance that, according to performance scholar Aldo Milohnić, has become 'part of the "lecture machine"' (2009: 36). As Milohnić discerns, a performative lecture machine creates a hybrid discursive situation, in which the academic realm and the realm of artistic production cross connect. In the case of *I Am 1984*, the intersecting lines of these encounters between dance, science and pedagogy coincide with the staging of the diagram.

Thematically, Matijević circles around the significant events of popular culture, media innovation and sports that marked the year 1984. At the same time, by connecting these information to her own biography, the performance construes a narrative network, displaying the vectors of subjectivation in the age of globalization. What gets highlighted in this process are, on the one hand, the technological apparatuses (computers, TV set, video games, film) and, on the other, questions of memory, fiction and biography. Drawing on the research by dance scholar Julia Wehren on choreography as a historiographic praxis, I argue that Matijević does not only perform knowledge but also engages in *performing history,* which can be qualified as a '(self) reflexive gesture' (2016: 54). As such, it is a gesture directed at activating, disseminating and preserving cultural memory and generating an archive with the means of the performance diagram.

With the stories of her wanting to enter the television, Isaac Asimov's robots and Billy Mitchell becoming the Pac-Man, the performance directs attention to instances in which the border between the human, the machine, the social and media apparatus becomes unstable and fluid. For a more speculative analysis, we could turn to the Italian philosopher Maurizio Lazzarato and his reflections on the concept of 'machinic enslavement'. It delineates a precise discursive framework to expand our notion of the performance diagram. Lazzarato develops his argumentation on the backdrop of Félix Guattari's critique of capitalist subjectivity[48] and offers a close reading of diagrammatic mutations inherent to the neoliberal society. Arguing that philosophers like Alain Badiou and Jacques Rancière have failed to connect capitalism to machinic enslavement, he asserts that 'these critical theories seem to have lost sight of what Marx had to say about the essentially machinic nature of capitalism' (2014: 13).

The concept of machinic enslavement denotes the ontological and societal mutation that result from the effect of the machine being material, semiotic,

---

[48] As Lazzarato explains, the production of subjectivity constitutes one of the most fundamental of capitalist concerns and 'implies the operations of mixed, signifying, symbolic, and asignifying semiotics' that, according to Guattari, 'operate in the economy, science, art, and machines' (2014: 17).

actual and virtual. Before it becomes a technique, the machine is diagrammatic and is inhabited by plans, formulas, equations and algorithmic commands. In a world increasingly regulated and governed by algorithmic protocols and the endless flow of digital data, we can identify a *diagrammatic effect* on the real. It is poignantly expressed in Lazzarato's thesis: 'Without diagrams, there is no capitalism' (2014: 90). Yet, breaking through the dualism separating words from images and subjects from objects, diagrams and diagrammatic imagination allow for envisioning new scenarios and possibilities for artistic creation and political action.

Applying these reflections to *I Am 1984*, we could argue that by performing the diagram, Matijević unwraps the network of societal and cultural forces that determine the vectors of subjectivation. Once activated and narrated, the diagram reveals the impact of media and pop cultural events on the semiotic process of becoming a subject in the postmodern, digital world.[49] For Guattari and Lazzarato, the diagrammatic function of capitalism results in subjugating bodies 'to the television machine as a user and consumer' (Lazzarato, 2014: 46). In our present moment, we might substitute television with social media and the Internet, but the idea remains the same: machinic and semiotic enslavement is induced through mass media apparatuses, cultural forms, educational systems, finances and consumption.

The performance diagram of *I Am 1984* multiplies the hybrid semiotic imprints, which, at the same time, are archives of the lecturing body in action. Accordingly, the performance unfolds a corporeality whose (ephemeral) presence goes through a process of self-documentation and becomes synonymous and coextensive with the diagram. Another possibility to engage with the diagram is to examine the relationality between the individual (signified by the various initials like 'B.M.' 'M.S.' or 'J.W.') and the social forces.

Following the argument of Erin Manning, who draws on Deleuze's notion of the diagram 'as a force of a coming-to-form that generates a shaping of experience', it could be asserted that the diagrammatic force is one 'that activates the collective individuation' and marks the point in which the body is *always more than one* (2012: 29). Moreover, in Manning's view, the choreographic field activates a diagrammatic practice surpassing representation and emerging in the form of a cartography of visceral intensities. This leads her to conclude that 'space-shaping is immanent to the activity of diagramming', which shows itself to be an 'emergent multiplicity' (2012: 134). In *I Am 1984*, the diagram works as the tool of narrative and visual multiplication as well as a device of self-archiving.

---

[49] The practice of *showing doing,* writes Milohnić, is especially relevant for autobiographical lecture performances (Milohnić, 2009: 36).

In this light, we can connect the performance of diagramming to that of archiving. If archiving is either 'a paranoic process about connecting with the past or (...) a system of *transforming simultaneously* past, present, and future' (Lepecki, 2016: 118), what comes to the fore in *I Am 1984* is precisely the ambiguous constellation between the body, history and memory. Although Matijević's choreography re-activates historical knowledge, I would assert that it does not function as a 'paranoid-melancholic compulsion to repeat' (Lepecki, 2016: 141). Instead, the performance sets in motion a transformational archive operating on the level of *affective kinetics*, staging and diagramming subjectivation on the backdrop of the force field of history.

Conclusion

The performance diagram in *Paradise Now* foregrounded an occult system of symbols and meanings whose origins are in the Kabbalah, the Ji-Ching and the system of Tantric Yoga. These different techniques fuse spiritual with visceral forces initiating a revolutionary turnover in the medium of performance. Barbara Matijević, on the other hand, engages in a diagrammatic choreography to display the dialectic cartography of subjectivation and subjugation. In both cases, the diagram figures as the primary instrument of performance-making. Yet, besides the obvious aesthetic differences in form and content, the two diagrams differ with regard to the staging.

The diagram of *Paradise Now* reads as a score of the performance; thus, it prefigures the scenic action. In *I Am 1984*, the diagram is an integral and central part of the performance, as it comes into existence during the lecture. Drawing on the idea of 'embodied diagrammatics', we could assert that the Living Theatre and Matijević generate 'new diagrammatic relations', which, in turn, activate a 'thinking in action' (Gansterer, Cocker and Greil, 2017: 321–322).

The diagrammatic paradigm in the two performances, I argue, serves to entangle poetics with politics. As Beck writes, a vital aspect of the poetics of the Living Theatre is to 'take language away from the governing class by subjecting it to imagination' (Beck, 1972: n.p.). In a similar way, Matijević develops a ludic and performative scenario that discloses apparatuses of subjugation, showing that 'curves, diagrams, and machines are indispensable components of enunciation, of non-human sites of partial subjectivation' (Lazzarato, 2014: 97). Having acquired the form of a vital instrument of performance-making, the two diagrams stir up imagination and create aesthetic conditions to challenge the capitalist machine. In such discursive configuration, the cosmopoetical diagram expands and transmutes into a cosmopolitical one.

Epilogue: The Poetic Surplus of Performance Diagrams

In an attempt to re-evaluate the visible aspect of performance (opsis) and its hybrid materiality, which represents a matter of secondary importance – the least artful and least valuable part of tragedy in Aristotle's *Poetics* – I have examined the concepts and practices of performance diagrams. In her deconstructive reading of the *Poetics*, French theatre scholar Florence Dupont shows how its reception since the eighteenth century had far-reaching consequences for the theatre. The most important one was the subordination of performance to the tyranny of the text and the disavowal of ludic and ritualistic elements (Dupont, 2007). With this in mind, I assert that the concept of the performance diagram creates a heuristic condition to rediscover and affirm precisely the ludic and ritualistic dimension of performance-making.

For Charles Sanders Peirce, one of the first thinkers to equate thinking with a diagrammatic activity, 'a diagram is a kind of icon' (1998: 13). It displays relations between elements that have no necessary connections. This argument implies that iconicity plays a central role in epistemic operations and cognition.[50] Therefore, diagrams and diagrammatic reasoning are indispensable elements of human experience and thinking. In his tripartite differentiation of signs (icon/index/symbol), which defines the discourse of semiotics, Peirce argues that icons display the similarity between them and their objects. *Diagrams-as-icons*, thus, operate within the regime of resemblance and make visible relations by a system of analogy.

As I have shown in Section 1, the architectural diagram by Vitruvius suggests that the space of theatre should correspond to the cosmological scheme and the twelve signs of the Zodiac. The precondition for the performance of the invocation ritual – which I examined regarding *Doctor Faustus* – follows the same doctrine of similarity and analogy. In the cases of Vitruvius and Marlowe, it mirrors the idea about the macrocosm being governed by the same forces and laws as the microcosm.

Recalling Foucault's[51] historiography of human sciences, which shows how the idea of similitude has been excluded from epistemology and how the Renaissance world of similarity was suppressed giving way to technologies of representation, classification and taxonomy, Sigrid Weigel asserts that Warburg's *Atlas* is envisaged as a pre-modern figuration of knowledge and art. It returns 'to the age preceding the separation of art and science as well as

---

[50] Drawing on Peirce, Sybille Krämer emphasizes that writing has a fundamental iconic nature, which allows us to consider dance notations and scripts as a hybrid (diagrammatic) composite situated between text and image.

[51] As Foucault notes, 'resemblance played a constructive role in the knowledge of Western culture' and in making things similar, 'the world is linked together like a chain' (2005: 19–21).

those of pictures and words' (2013: 9). The same could be said of Artaud's spells and the diagram of *Paradise Now*. Although it might not be evident at first in the *I Am 1984* diagram, I am arguing that it also weaves a web of analogies, correspondences and similarities between historical events and the biography of the performer.

With this in mind, we can conclude that the performance diagrams examined in this Element unfold a poetic texture composed of images, words and lines, thus, can be seen as a *survival and return of similitude*. In a short essay entitled *On the Mimetic Faculty* (*Über das mimetische Vermögen*, Ger. Orig.), Walter Benjamin outlines his theory of the similar that he links to mimetic activity. Although he does not explicitly write about diagrams, Benjamin's notion of *nonsensuous similarity*, which he relates to practices of astrology and cultic dances, can delineate a conceptual framework to comprehend how diagrams activate a regime of similitude and analogy.

As Benjamin writes, the mimetic faculty central to the doctrine of 'correspondences and analogies' (2002: 124) is barely present in modern societies because magic seems to be liquidated. The identity between the macrocosm and microsome underlying the concept of similitude comes to the fore in ancient astrology, which is the source of both speaking and writing.[52] Despite the triumph of rationality and scientism, we see that theological, mythological and occult ideas continue to influence human imagination and poetics. Interpreting performance diagrams as manifestations of such a nonsensuous similarity in which theological, metaphysical and ritualistic formulas/symbols interact, we can assert that their poetic surplus equals the restitution of analogy and mythological imagination. On the other hand, the affirmation of diagrams also signals 'a comeback of an interest in iconicity', which can be used to examine the visuality of performance (Stjernfelt, 2007: 60).

Another thread connecting the examples of performance diagrams is the concept of *ars combinatoria*, which translates as an art of combination. It consists of a practice in which letters or numbers are subjected to a process of rearrangement and montage.[53] While the chance method is an obvious element in Ji-Ching and thereby plays an important role in the *Paradise Now* diagram,

---

[52] In a detailed study of astrological and esoteric motifs in Benjamin's work, Wolfgang Bock shows how 'the connection between the stars, writing, reading and language have their root in mystic Judaism' (1999: 33).

[53] The term *ars combinatoria* relates to the Catalan philosopher, theologian and poet Ramon Llul (1232–1316) who had created a philosophical system based on combinatorial operations. The primary characteristics of *ars combinatoria* can be described as follows: 'The breaking down of compound concepts into simple and irreducible notions, the use of letters and symbols to represent simple notions, the mechanization of conceptual combination by means of movable figures or diagrams' (Rossi, 2006: 32).

the *poetics of permutation* is central to the kabbalistic technique known as Gematria, something we have come across in the spells Artaud sent from Ireland.

At the same time, Camillo's *Theatre of Memory* and Warburg's *Atlas* demonstrate the ability to shift images, symbols and text, giving up the idea of a 'fixed configuration' (Didi-Huberman, 2017: 301). Such a logic centred around the play of permutation governs also the diagram of *I Am 1984*, emerging as a result of an unfolding of diagrammatic constellations. Since the method of *ars combinatoria* was a vital part of Renaissance Neoplatonism, it directly relates to the ritualistic practice embodied in *Doctor Faustus'* diagram.

In the context of a structuralist theory of dramaturgy, the idea of *ars combinatoria* comes to the fore in Etienne Souriau's book on 20,000 dramatic situations (*Les deux cent mille situations dramatiques* Fr. Orig.). He considers the idea that dramatic situations should be modelled according to a combination of six basic dramatic functions. More precisely, Souriau conceives of the dramatic events as a constellation and fluctuation of desire between characters who oppose each other and who embody one of the six functions. To each of the dramatic functions, Souriau attaches an astrological sign, 'which results in an astonishing and effective sort of astrological, analytical algebra for denoting the forces in the characters and their relationship in the situation' (Hahn, 1951: 267). In Souriau's own words: 'It is the structural diagram drawn, in a given moment of the action, by a system of forces (. . .) present in the microcosm, stellar centre of the theatrical universe; and incarnated, undergone or animated by the principal personages of this moment of the action' (Souriau in Hahn, 1951: 266).

Another point of intersection is the concept and practice of the diagram understood as an instrument of ideation, classification and construction of knowledge. At the same time, by connecting and constellating spaces and images, performance diagrams also acquire the function of archives. Writing about the power of images and mnemonic places in the work of Ramon Llul, Paolo Rossi argues that 'the art of memory appeared to be closely linked with the idea of a secret art', which can be understood as 'a combination of conventional mnemotechnical rules with formulaic invocations, mystical figures and magical prayers' (2006: 12).

Besides Peirce, who reflects on the diagram having in mind its didactic and pedagogical function in mathematics and logic, the other two philosophers responsible for the affirmation of contemporary diagrammatic thinking are Deleuze and Guattari. However, compared to Peirce, the source of the diagram for them is not only in algebra and geometry but in the hermetic and poetic tradition of perennial philosophy that flourished during the Renaissance.

A superficial look into the manuscripts of authors like Llul, Ficino, Mirandola, Agrippa, Dee or Paracelsus reveals numerous diagrams depicting the correspondence between astrological signs and body parts, ritualistic formulas or magic omens as protection tools against evil spirits.

In his study on the embeddedness of Deleuze's thinking in the hermetic tradition, Joshua Ramey argues that the French philosopher 'stands as a contemporary avatar of Western esoteric or "hermetic" thought, and must be understood as a contemporary, nonidentical repetition of this tradition' (2012: 3). With a reference to Artaud's *Theatre of Cruelty*, Ramey begins his book by connecting the *Body without Organs* with the affirmation of the spiritual significance of corporeality and materiality in Deleuze's philosophy. In the context of the revival of hermetic ideas, Ramey discusses the significance of diagrams for Deleuze. As he writes, their function is 'to map lines of force of cosmic rhythms', implying a 'demiurgic and theandric' quality of diagrams in the arts. (2012: 165)

The sources of performance diagrams are: the structuralist-semiotic discourse, the hermetic tradition and the vectors of affective corporeality. The poetic surplus is the consequence of the dynamic entanglement of scientific/ mathematical reasoning and mythological thinking premised on similarity and analogy. Hence, the poetics of performance diagrams allow us to traverse the epistemic, ontological and social order established on a system of dichotomies and representations.[54]

Furthermore, the poetics of performance diagrams epitomizes an attempt to formulate a hybrid and *nomadic* topology of theatre-making that can delineate new theoretical approaches to visuality, spatiality and the historiography of performance.[55] In short, performance diagrams offer 'new forms of poetic imagination' allowing for multiple narratives to circulate and reorganize the relation between the stage and the audience (Moro, 2021: 167). I argue that the turn and re-turn to diagrams unfold along a discursive trajectory similar to the one set by Hans Thies-Lehmann in his reflections on postdramatic forms of theatre. For Thies-Lehmann, performance studies can challenge the supremacy of language and text by shifting the focus to spatiality, mediality and corporeality.

---

[54] Perhaps, the concept of performance diagrams can be utilized to establish new relations between performance studies and the theoretical approach developed within the discourse of new materialism.

[55] In her pioneering work on visuality in theatre, Bonnie Marranca writes about the Richard Foreman's performance *Pandering to the masse* as presenting a 'diagrammatic reality' (1996: 9). The *theatre of images*, Marranca asserts, brought the preforming and the visual arts to a new understanding of performance, which moved away from conventional text-based dramaturgy. As a consequence, the narrative and dramaturgical potentialities of images have gained a new (poetic) relevance.

From a *cosmopolitical* perspective, theatre and dance diagrams, as we discussed them in Section 3, reveal relations of power intrinsic to the neoliberal machinic and its tracks of algorithmic enslavement. Drawing an analogy to mapping and counter-mapping tactics, diagrams activated in and by performances can chart new territories of collectivity and solidarity. As a 'duality composed of tracing and mapping', the diagram renders visible and sensible the process of graphic translation that can be vital to comprehend the 'undiscovered spaces' of performance (Zdebik, 2012: 109) If it is reasonable to believe that performance diagrams function like an 'autopoietic machine', we could ask if we can consider them to act as vectors of sociopolitical transformation (Guattari, 1995: 44). In other words, what kind of sociality can be imagined departing from a diagrammatic poetics of performance?

Arguing finally that their power lies in the potentiality of proliferating an aesthetic practice that breaks through representation and the ontological, existential and political dichotomies, diagrams set the stage to rethink our relationship not only between humans but also between us and our endangered environments. In that way, the cosmopoetic and cosmopolitical concepts of performance diagrams establish a discursive framework to critically redraw the borders between the human and the non-human, seeking for ethical, ecological intersections and imagining alternative trajectories of togetherness.

References

Agrippa, H. C. (2021). *Three Books on Occult Philosophy*. Translated by Eric Purdue. Rochester: Inner Traditions.

Antliff, A. (2015). Poetic Tension, Aesthetic Cruelty: Paul Goodman, Antonin Artaud and the Living Theatre. *Anarchist Modernities*, No. 1&2, pp. 3–30.

Aristoteles. (2006). *Poetics*. Translated by Joe Sachs. Newburyport: Focus.

Artaud, A. (1965). *Artaud Anthology*. Translated by Jack Hirschman. San Francisco: City Light Books.

Artaud, A. (1988). *Selected Writings*. Translated by Helen Weaver. Los Angeles: University of California Press.

Artaud, A. (1999). *Collected Works. Volume Four*. Translated by Victor Corti. London: John Calder.

Artaud, A. (2016). *50 Drawings to Murder Magic*. Translated by Donald Nichlson-Smith. New York: Seagull books.

Barber, S. (2019). *Artaud 1937 Apocalypse: Letters from Ireland by Antonin Artaud*. Zürich: Diaphanes.

Beck, J. (1972). *The life of the Theatre: The Relation of the Artist to the Struggle of the People*. San Francisco: City Lights.

Benjamin, W. (2002). *Medienästhetische Schriften*. Frankfurt: Suhrkamp Verlag.

Billeter, E. (1968). *The Living Theatre, Paradise Now: Ein Bericht in Wort und Bild*. Bern: Benteli Verlag.

Bing, G. (1993). Aby M. Warburg. In Uwe Flackner, Robert Galitz, Claudia Naber, et al., eds. *Aby M. Warburg : Bildersammlung zur Geschichte von Sternglaube und Sternkunde im Hamburger Planetarium*. Hamburg: Dölling und Galitz Verlag. pp. 14–23.

Blackbourn, W. (1978). Heavenly Words: Marlow's Faustus as a Renaissance Magician. *English Studies in Canada*, Vol. 4, No. 1, Spring, pp. 1–14.

Bock, W. (1999). *Die Rettung der Nacht: Sterne, Melancholie und Messiansmus*. Bielefeld: Aisthesis.

Bogen, S. and Thürlemann, F. (2003). Jenseits der Opposition von Text und Bild. Überlegungen zu einer Theorie des Diagramms und des Diagrammatischen. In A. Patschovsky, ed., *Die Bildwelt der Diagramme Joachims von Fiore: zur Medialität religiös-politischer Programme im Mittelalter*. Stuttgart: Jan Thorbecke Verlag. pp. 1–22.

Brandstetter, G. (2015). *Poetics of Dance: Body, Image and Space in the Historic Avant-Gardes*. Translated by Elena Polzer. Oxford: Oxford University Press.

Brandstetter, G., Hoffman, F. and Maar, K., eds. (2010). *Notationen und Choreografisches Denken*. Freiburg: Rombach Verlag.

Bronfen, E. (2018). *Crossmappings: On Visual Culture*. London: I.B. Tauris.

Butler, E. M. (1949). *Ritual Magic*. London: Cambridge University Press.

Campion, N. (2009). *History of Western Astrology Volume I: The Ancient World*. London: Continuum.

Crespi, P. (2022). Rudolf's Laban Diagrammatics: Moving Structures for Movement-Thinking. *Performance Research*, Vol. 27, No. 8, pp. 108–116.

Critchlow, K. (2011a). *The Hidden Geometry of Flowers: Living Rhythms Form and Number*. Edinburgh: Floris Books.

Critchlow, K. (2011b). *Islamic Patterns: An Analytical and Cosmological Approach*. London: Thames and Hudson.

Cull, L. (2013). *Theatre of Immanence: Deleuze and the Ethics of Performance*. London: Palgrave Macmillan.

Davies, O. (2009). *Grimoires: A History of Magic Books*. Oxford: Oxford University Press.

De Rolley, T. M. (2016). Putting the Devil on the Map: Demonology and Cosmography in the Renaissance. In K. Vermeir and J. Regier, eds., *Boundaries, Extents and Circulations: Space and Spatiality in Early Modern Philosophy*. Berlin: Springer. pp. 179–209.

Degani-Raz, I. (2008). Diagrams, Formalism, and Structural Homology in Beckett's Come and Go. *Journal of Dramatic Theory and Criticism*, Vol. 22, No. 2, Spring, pp. 133–146.

Degani-Raz, I. (2021). Spatial Diagrams and Geometrical Reasoning in Theatre. *Semiotica. Journal of the International Association for Semiotic Studies*, Vol. 2021, No.239, pp. 2–24.

Deleuze, G. (1988). *Foucault*. Translated by Seán Hand. Minneapolis: University of Minnesota Press.

Deleuze, G. (2007). *Francis Bacon: The Logic of Sensation*. Translated by Daniel W. Smith. London and New York: Continuum.

Deleuze, G. and Guattari, F. (2004). *A Thousand Plateaus: Capitalism and Schizophrenia*. Translated by Brian Massumi. New York: Continuum.

Derrida, J. (1981). *Dissemination*. Translated by Barbara Johnson. Chicago: University of Chicago Press.

Derrida, J. (1998). To Unsense the Subjectile. In P. Thévenine and J. Derrida, eds., *The Secret Art of Antonin Artaud*. Translated by Mary Ann Caws. Massachusetts: The MIT Press. pp. 59–157.

Didi-Huberman, G. (2017). *Surviving Image: Phantoms of Time and Time of Phantoms: Aby Warburg's History of Art*. Translated by Harvey L. Mendelsohn. Philadelphia: The Pennsylvania State University Press.

Dupont, F. (2007). *Aristote ou le vampire du théâtre occidental*. Paris: Aubier.

Foucault, M. (2005). *The Order of Things: An Archaeology of Human Sciences*. Translated by Alan Sheridan. London: Routledge.

Franko, M. (2019). *Choreographing Discourse: A Mark Franko Reader*. New York: Routledge.

Gansterer, N., Cocker, E. and Greil, M., eds. (2017). *Choreo-Graphic Figures: Deviations from the Line*. Vienna: Die Angewandte University Press.

Gardner, T. (2003). Breathing's Hieroglyhics. *Performance Research*, Vol. 8, No. 2, pp. 109–116.

Giardino, V. (2016). Behind the Diagrams: Cognitive Issues and Open Problems. In S. Krämer and C. Ljungberg, eds., *Thinking with Diagrams: The Semiotic Basis of Human Cognition*. Berlin: Walter de Gruyter. pp. 77–103.

Glissant, É. (1997). *Poetics of Relation*. Translated by Betsy Wing. Ann Arbor: University of Michigan Press.

Guattari, F. (1995). *Chaosmosis: An Ethico-Aesthetic Paradigm*. Translated by Paul Bains and Juliana Pefanis. Indianapolis: Indiana University Press.

Gebhardt Fink, S. and Rust, D. (2022). Mapping and Crossmapping the History of Performance Art in Switzerland through Collective Research for Deviant Understandings. *Performance Research*, Vol. 27, No. 8, pp. 89–97.

Gough, R. (2022). A Puzzle of Diagrams (Incorrect Collective Noun/ Incomplete Collection). *Performance Research*, Vol. 27, No. 8, pp. 77–80.

Gregg, M. and Seigworth, G. J., eds. (2010). *The Affective Theory Reader*. Durham: Duke University Press.

Grossman, E. (2016). *50 Drawings to Murder Magic*. Translated by Donald Nicholson-Smith. London: Seagull Books.

Hahn, P. (1951). Review. *Educational Theatre Journal*, Vol. 3, No. 3, pp. 266–268.

Hamburger, J. F. (2020). *Diagramming Devotion: Berthold of Nuremberg's Transformation of Hrabanus Maurus's Poems in the Praise of the Cross*. Chicago: The University of Chicago Press.

Harren, N. (2022). The Time of Diagrams: A Theory of Notation. *Performance Research*, Vol. 27, No. 8, pp. 145–152.

Harries, K. (2002). Sphere and Cross: Vitruvian Reflections on the Pantheon Type. In G. Dodds and R. Tavernor, eds., *Body and Building: Essays on the Changing Relation of Body and Architecture*. Massachusetts: The MIT Press.

Heard, E. (2006). Space, Signs and Artaud's Hieroglyphic Body. *Performance Research*, Vol. 11, No. 1, pp. 40–53.

Hewitt, A. (2005). *Social Choreography: Ideology as Performance in Dance and Everyday Movements*. Durham: Duke University Press.

Horvath, G. D. (2017). *Theatre, Magic and Philosophy: William Shakespeare, John Dee and the Italian Legacy*. New York: Routledge.

Janowitz, N. (2002). *Icons of Power: Ritual Practices in Late Antiquity.* State College: Penn University Press.

Johnson, C. D. (2012). *Memory, Metaphor and Aby Warburg's Atlas of Images.* New York: Cornell University Press.

Khanna, M. (1994). *Yantra: The Tantric Symbol of Cosmic Unity.* London: Thames and Hudson.

Klassen, F. (2013). *The Transformation of Magic: Illicit Learned Magic in the Later Middle Ages and Renaissance.* Pennsylvania: Pennsylvania State University.

Krämer, S. (2009). Operative Bildlichkeit. Von der 'Grammatologie' zu einer Diagrammatologie? Reflexion über erkennendes 'Sehen'. In M. Heßler and D. Mersch, eds., *Logik des Bildlichen: Zur Kritik der ikonischen Vernunft.* Bielefeld: Transcript. pp. 94–123.

Krämer, S. (2016). *Figuration, Anschaulichkeit, Erkenntnis.* Frankfurt: Suhrkamp.

Krämer, S. and Ljungberg, C., eds. (2016). *Thinking with Diagrams: The Semiotic Basis of Human Cognition.* Berlin: Walter de Gruyter.

Lazardzig, J., Tkaczyk, V. and Warstat, M. (2012). *Theaterhistoriografie. Eine Einführung.* Tübingen: A Francke Verlag.

Lazzarato, M. (2014). *Signs and Machines: Capitalism and the Production of Subjectivity.* Los Angeles: Semiotext(e).

Leach, N. (2005). *Vitruvius Crucifixus*: Architecture, Mimesis, and the Death Instinct. In G. Dodds and R. Tavernor, eds., *Body and Building: Essays on the Changing Relation of Body and Architecture.* Massachusetts: MIT Press. pp. 210–226

Lehmann, H. T. (2016). *Tragedy and Dramatic Theatre.* Translated by Erik Butler. London: Routledge.

Lehrich, C. I. (2003). *The Language of Demons and Angels: Cornelius Agrippa 's Occult Philosophy.* Leiden: Brill.

Lepecki, A. (2016). *Singularities: Dance in the Age of Performance.* New York: Routledge.

Lingan, E. B. (2014). *The Theatre of the Occult Revival: Alternative Spiritual Performance from 1875 to the Present.* London: Palgrave Macmillan.

Louppe, L., ed. (1994). *Traces of Dance: Drawings and Notations of Choreographers.* Paris: Dis Voir.

Magness, J. (2005). Heaven on Earth: Helios and the Zodiac Cycle in Ancient Palestinian Synagogues. *Dumbarton Oaks Papers*, Vol. 59, pp. 1–52.

Malina, J. (2012). *The Piscator Notebooks.* New York: Routledge.

Manning, E. (2012). *Always More Than One.* Durham: Duke University Press.

Marlowe, C. (2003). *The Complete Plays.* London: Penguin Books.

Marranca, B. (1996). *The Theatre of Images*. New York: PAJ.

Matheson, N. (2018). *Surrealism and the Gothic Castles of the Interior.* London: Routledge.

Mcalindon, T. (1994). Doctor Faustus: Grounded in Astrology. *Literature & Theology*, Vol. 8, No. 4, pp. 384–393.

McEwen, I. K. (2003). *Vitruvius: Writing the Body of Architecture*. London: MIT Press.

Mebane, J. S. (1992). *Renaissance Magic and the Return of the Golden Age: The Occult Tradition and Marlowe, Jonson, and Shakespeare.* Lincoln: University of Nebraska Press.

Miller, J. (1986). *Measures of Wisdom: The Cosmic Dance in Classical and Christian Antiquity.* Toronto: University of Toronto Press.

Milohnić, A. (2009). Performing Lecture Machine. In K. Jentjens and J. Dirksen, eds., *Lecture Performance*, Köln and Belgrade: Revolver/Museum of Contemporary Art.

Mirčev, A. (2021). Diagrammatic Dramaturgies: Navigations between Theory and Movement. In E. Fischer-Lichte, T. Jost and Ch. Weiler, eds., *Dramaturgies of Interweaving: Engaging Audiences in an Entangled World*. London: Routledge. pp. 47–60.

Mirčev, A. (2022). Editorial: Diagramming Performances. *Performance Research*, Vol. 27, No. 8, pp. 1–09.

Mee, C. L. (1962). The Beck's Living Theatre. *The Tulane Drama Review*, Vol. 7, No. 2 (Winter), pp. 194–205.

Moro, S. (2021). *Poetic Cartography: Mapping Paradigms Modern in Contemporary Art.* New York: Routledge.

Mullarkey, J. (2006). *Post-Continental philosophy: An Outline.* New York: Continuum.

Müller, K. (2008). *Visuelle Weltaneignung: Astronomische und kosmologische Diagramme in Handschriften des Mittelalters.* Göttingen: V andenhoeck& Ruprecht.

Murray, R. (2014). *Antonin Artaud: The Scum of the Soul.* London: Palgrave Macmillan.

Naber, C. (1993). Einleitung. In Uwe Flackner, Robert Galitz, Claudia Naber, et al. eds., *Aby M. Warburg: Bildersammlung zur Geschichte von Sternglaube und Sternkunde im Hamburger Planetarium*. Hamburg: Dölling und Galitz Verlag. pp. 10–12.

Paar, J. (1971). *Tamburlaine's Malady and Essays on Astrology in Elizabethan Drama.* Connecticut: Greenwood Press.

Peirce, C. S. (1998). *The Essential Peirce: Selected Philosophical Writings. Volume 2 (1893–1913).* Indianapolis: Indiana University Press.

Pellerin, P.-A. (2018). Theatre and Protest in 1968: An Interview with Judith Malina, Co-founder of the Living Theatre, *Theatre Topics*, Vol. 28, No. 2, pp. 1–6.

Penner, J. (2014). On Aggro Performance: Audience Participation and the Dystopian Response to the Living Theatre's *Paradise Now. Comparative Drama*, Vol. 48, No. 1&2, Spring & Summer, pp. 75–92.

Plato (2009). *Timaeus and Critias*. Translated by Robin Waterfield. Oxford: Oxford University Press.

Rainer, L. (2017). *On the Threshold of Knowing: Lectures and Performance in Art and Academia*. Bielefeld: Transcript.

Ramey, J. (2012). *The Hermetic Deleuze: Philosophy and Spiritual Ordeal*. Durham: Duke University Press.

Rossi, P. (2006). *Logic and the Art of Memory: The Quest for a Universal Language*. London: Continuum.

Rowell, M. (2017). Images of Cruelty: The Drawings of Antonin Artaud. In Margit Rowell, ed., *Antonin Artaud: Works on Paper*. New York: The Museum of Modern Art. pp. 11–17.

Ruprecht, L. (2019). *Gestural Imaginaries: Dance and Cultural Theory in the Early Twentieth Century*. Oxford: Oxford University Press.

Schmidt-Burkhardt, A. (2012). *Die Kunst der Diagrammatik: Perspektiven eines neuen bildwissenschaftlichen Paradigmas*. Bielefeld: Transcript Verlag.

Schneider, R. (2011). *Performing Remains: Art and War in Times of Theatrical Reenactment*. London: Routledge.

Scholem, G. (1954). *Major Trends in Jewish Mysticism*. New York: Schocken Books.

Scholem, G. (1969). *On the Kabbalah and Its Symbolism*. New York: Schocken Books.

Schwan, H. A. (2022). *Schrift im Raum: Korrelationen von Tanz un Schreiben bei Trisha Brown, Jan Fabre und William Forsythe*. Bielefeld: Transcript Verlag.

Sherman, B. (2020). Under the Sign of Mnemosyne. In R. Ohr and A. Heil, eds., *Aby Warburg Bilderatlas Mnemosyne – The Original*. Berlin: Hatje Catz Verlag. pp. 8–9.

Sofer, A. (2009). How to Do Things with Demons: Conjuring Performatives in Doctor Faustus. *Theatre Journal*, Vol. 61, No. 1, pp. 1–21.

Stjernfelt, F. (2007). *Diagrammatology: An Investigation on the Borderlines of Phenomenology, Ontology, and Semiotics*. Berlin: Springer.

Summers, D. (2003). *Real Spaces: World Art History and the Rise of Western Modernism*. London: Phaidon Press.

Thévenine, P. (1998). The Search for a Lost World. In P. Thévenine and J. Derrida, eds., *The Secret Art of Antonin Artaud*. Translated by Mary Ann Caws. London: The MIT Press. pp. 1–59.

Twitchin, M. (2016). *The Theatre of Death – The Uncanny in Mimesis: Tadeusz Kantor, Aby Warburg, and an Iconology of the Actor*. London: Palgrave Macmillan.

Wallen, L. and Brezjek, T. (2018). *The Model as Performance: Staging Space in Theatre and Architecture*. London: Bloomsbury Methuen Drama.

Weigel, S. (2013). Epistemology of Wandering, Tree and Taxonomy. *Images Re-vue*, Hors-série 4 | document 15.

Weigel, S. (2015). *Grammatologie der Bilder*. Frankfurt: Suhrkamp.

Weigel, S. and Treml, M. (2010). Einleitung. In M. Treml, S. Weigel and P. Ladwig, eds., *Aby Warburg. Werke in einem Band*. Frankfurt: Suhrkamp. pp. 9–31.

Vesely, D. (2002). The Architectonics of Embodiment. In G. Dodds and R. Tavernor, eds., *Body and Building: Essays on the Changing Relation of Body and Architecture*. London: The MIT Press, pp. 28–43.

The Living Theatre. (1969). Paradise Now: Notes. *The Drama Review: TDR*, Vol. 13, No. 3 (Spring), pp. 90–107.

Vitruvius. (2001). *Ten Books on Architecture*. Translated by Ingrid D. Rowland. Cambridge: Cambridge University Press.

Vitruvius. (1914). *The Ten books on architecture*. Translated by Morris Hicky Morgan. Harvard: Harvard University Press.

Warburg, A. (1939). A Lecture on Serpent Ritual. *Journal of the Warburg Institute*, Vol. 2, No. 4, pp. 277–292.

Warburg, A. (1999). *The Renewal of Pagan Antiquity: Contributions to the Cultural History of the European Renaissance*. Translated by David Britt. Los Angeles: Getty Institute for the History of Art and the Humanities.

Warburg, A. (2010). M. Treml, S. Weigel and P. Ladwig, eds., *Aby Warburg: Werke in einem Band*. Berlin: Suhrkamp Verlag.

Warburg, A. (2012). *Gesammelte Schriften. Bilderatlas Mnemosyne*. Berlin: Akademie Verlag.

Wedepohl, C. (2005). Ideengeographie. Ein Versuch zu Aby Warburgs ʹWanderstraßen der Kultur.ʹ In H. Mitterbauer and K. Scherke, eds., *Entgrenzte Räume*. Wien: Passagen Verlag. pp. 227–255.

Wedepohl, C. (2020). The Making of Warburg's Bilderatlas Mnemosyne. In R. Ohr and A. Heil, eds., *Aby Warburg Bilderatlas Mnemosyne –The Original*. Berlin: Hatje Catz Verlag. pp. 14–19.

Wehren, J. (2016). *Körper als Archiv in Bewegung: Choreografie als historiografische Praxis*. Bielefeld: Transcript Verlag.

Willes, Wiles, D. (1997). *Tragedy in Athens: Performance Space and Theatrical Meaning*. Cambridge: Cambridge University Press.

Willes, Wiles D. (2003). *A Short History of Western Performance Space*. Cambridge: Cambridge University Press.

Yates, F. A. (1969). *Theatre of the World*. London: Routledge.

Yates, F. A. (1999). *Selected Works. Volume III. The Art of Memory*. London: Routledge.

Zdebik, J. (2012). *Deleuze and the Diagram: Aesthetic Threads in Visual Organization*. New York: Continuum.

Zumbusch, C. (2004). *Wissenschaft in Bildern: Symbol und dialektisches Bild in Aby Warburg's Mnemosyne-Atlas und Walter Benjamin's Passagenwerk*. Berlin: Akademie Verlag.

About the Author

Andrej Mirčev is an academic and dramaturge. He received his PhD from Freie Universität Berlin. In 2018 he was fellow at the International Center *Interweaving Performance Cultures* in Berlin. His research focus is: spatial theory, intermediality, performance and memory. Mircev is Guest Professor at the University of Arts (UdK) in Berlin.

Cambridge Elements ☰

Contemporary Performance Texts

Senior Editor

Fintan Walsh

Birkbeck, University of London

Fintan Walsh is Professor of Performing Arts and Humanities at Birkbeck, University of London, where he is Head of the School of Creative Arts, Culture and Communication and Director of Birkbeck Centre for Contemporary Theatre. He is a former Senior Editor of *Theatre Research International.*

Associate Editors

Duška Radosavljević

Royal Central School of Speech and Drama, University of London

Duška Radosavljević is a Professorial Research Fellow at the Royal Central School of Speech and Drama. Her work has received the David Bradby Research Prize (2015), the Elliott Hayes Award for Dramaturgy (2022) and the ATHE-ASTR Award for Digital Scholarship

Caridad Svich

Rutgers University

Caridad Svich is a playwright and translator. She teaches creative writing and playwriting in the English Department at Rutgers University-New Brunswick.

Advisory Board

Siân Adiseshiah, *Loughborough University*

Helena Grehan, *Western Australian Academy of Performing Arts*

Ameet Parameswaran, *Jawaharlal Nehru University*

Synne Behrndt, *Stockholm University of the Arts*

Jay Pather, *University of Cape Town*

Sodja Zupanc Lotker, *The Academy of Performing Arts in Prague (DAMU)*

Peter M. Boenisch, *Aarhus University*

Hayato Kosuge, *Keio University*

Edward Ziter, *NYU Tisch School of the Arts*

Milena Gras Kleiner, *Pontificia Universidad Católica de Chile*

Savas Patsalidis, *Aristotle University, Thessaloniki, Greece*

Harvey Young, *College of Fine Arts, Boston University*

About the Series

Contemporary Performance Texts responds to the evolution of the form, role and meaning of text in theatre and performance in the late twentieth and twenty-first centuries, by publishing Elements that explore the generation of text for performance, its uses in performance, and its varied modes of reception and documentation.

Cambridge Elements ≡

Contemporary Performance Texts

Printed in the United States
by Baker & Taylor Publisher Services